Levin's Laws

Levin's Laws

Tactics for Winning Without Intimidation

Edward Levin

M. Evans and Company, Inc.   NEW YORK

Library of Congress Cataloging in Publication Data

Levin, Edward.
  Levin's laws.

  1. Negotiation. I. Title.
HD38.L3973   158   79-21192
ISBN 0-87131-308-1

M. Evans and Company, Inc.
216 East 49 Street
New York, New York 10017

Design by Robert Bull

Manufactured in the United States of America

9 8 7 6 5 4 3 2 1

To my family, who taught me all about bargaining.

Contents

One

The Laws of
Bargaining

*P*EOPLE WORRY THAT they're not as tough or as smart as those with whom they have to keep negotiating. More often than not they think "the other guy" has the ability to walk all over them. "You're a professional, Ed," they say. "Tell me what to do about this problem with my directors" (or my ex-husband or wife, my landlord, my boss, my secretary). I tell them it's not necessarily a matter of being shrewd or tough, though that may help. It's a matter of evening out the percentages so that you know as much as the people who try to take advantage of you. To get what you want out of a situation where there are two sides, you have to learn the techniques of problem solving. You have to understand what it means to negotiate an argument so that you get what you want. And you have to understand and be able to choose the tactics that will work. It's only fair that you should know how to take care of yourself as well as the other guy does.

The tactics that win have nothing to do with belligerence. I've seen this proved again and again. Bullies who blaze their way through life, intimidating and browbeating, really don't know how to take care of themselves at all. What they do is set themselves up as rats. People will do whatever they can to get rid of rats. You have to play the game smart, not rough.

I've had to learn how to work both sides of an argument. I've been a union man who has worked as a railroad freight conductor, a tugboat fireman, and a longshoreman loading banana boats. I've known management's side: I studied collective bargaining, labor relations, and industrial administration at Oxford, Yale, and Cornell. I've been on both sides and now I'm working the middle as a professional mediator and arbitrator. The friends and colleagues who ask my advice think that because I'm a professional mediator, I know something ordinary citizens don't. They think we professionals win because we have some magic way of manipulating people in our favor. I don't have any magic. What I have is a system. It's a system that works in the living room the same way it works at the bargaining table. Because what happens in the living room is what happens at the bargaining table. People argue over conflicting goals. Some win, some do not.

The principles are the same whatever the conflict. Whether you're battling with a neighbor over the lawnmower or with your boss over a raise, the strategies and tactics you apply determine what you come out with. It doesn't matter if you think your neighbor or boss has better grounds than you do; it's which of you handles himself better that counts. Nor does it matter if the other person is out to kill. We all know people who are out for blood. Just remember, they can't make mincemeat of you if you know how to disarm them.

I repeat, the point of a fight, in professional bargaining and in daily personal warfare, is to take care of yourself so you get what you want.

I'm going to teach you the system. It boils down to six fundamentals:

1. Analyze the situation.
2. Decide on your goals and alternatives.
3. Evaluate your adversary.
4. Strategize your approach.
5. Do your homework.
6. Apply the tactics that will get you where you want to be.

The six steps I've outlined are shorthand for scores of fascinating methods and skills. Learning them can change your life. I've seen it happen to friends and students who have suddenly gained fresh insights into the things that happen to them every day. Mastering the tactics of backstage bargaining teaches you to think fast on your feet. It teaches you how to use other people to protect yourself, how to invent new options, and how to take advantage of opportunities you didn't know existed.

You will learn the techniques used by the most successful bargainers and negotiators in the world, the headline makers who got where they are because they know how to bring conflict to the point where they're in the driver's seat. You will understand why people act as they do. You will learn how to read their minds and how to outthink them. If you get no more out of this book than learning how to outthink your opponent in a fight, you will be far ahead of the game.

Somebody has to be out front. Why not you?

Two

The Nature of Conflict

*C*ONFLICT OPENS DOORS. When people reach the point where they are disagreeing openly, there is a chance for resolution. They can talk about what's wrong—money, service, fairness, whatever—and look for ways to make changes for the better. Disagreement is one of the best ways in the world to turn the tide and improve unsatisfactory conditions.

People are constantly dissatisfied. That's why there is constant dissension. The point is to recognize that life is a series of conflicts, and conflict is opportunity—if you know how to use it.

As a professional, I can tell you one thing for sure. Most people have no idea how to bring off a winning fight without getting themselves into deeper snarls than they had in the first place. Everybody gets into arguments. Different people have different goals and points of view and it's human nature to disagree. But managing a fight so the payoff is in your favor is hard to bring off. Knowing how to bargain takes skill and special techniques. These have to be learned.

Of course, I didn't know all this when I first went into professional dispute settlement. In fact, I'd say I was pretty bad for the first few years. Made all the mistakes in the book. But because I was in the position of being an outsider involved in a great many more disagreements than the average person—disagreements that were actually defined as such—I received a fast and thorough education in the fine art of fighting. And there's nothing in the rules that says I can't pass that education along to you.

One thing I've learned is that conflict comes in all shapes and sizes, from cosmic warfare to spats at the breakfast table. Disagreements are as much a way of life for international diplomats and politicians as they are for a husband and wife or a student versus the faculty. We know that unions and companies quarrel all the time about money, power, rights, service. How many times have you gotten into arguments over the same things with a car dealer, your landlord, the TV repairman?

How do you tell which conflicts are important? Any fight is major to the people who are in it up to here. A family bout over where to take a vacation maybe won't change the world, but it can be a hotter issue by far to the battlers than the global negotiations going on in Washington or Geneva. I've seen labor and management teams get just as hot under the collar over a couple of thousand dollars as businessmen arguing in the millions. The only difference is some added-on zeros. There is a lesson in that, too: The fastest way to make an enemy is to tell somebody he's getting all lathered up over a piddling problem and he ought to be concerning himself with the starving nations instead.

Levin's Law: *Conflict is opportunity. Do not underestimate the chance it gives you for change.*

The Cat's Cradle of Conflict

A fight may wind up being beneficial or destructive to one or both sides, or just plain fruitless all around. It depends on what's done to and by both parties during combat: how one manipulates the other, the negotiating and bargaining skills each has in his corner, the chivying and maneuvering that goes on. And more. There's a whole network of variables and influences in bargaining that are as inseparable as a tangle of wire hangers in the coat closet.

We all see and treat the rest of the world in the light of our own social, cultural, and economic backgrounds. We react unconsciously to gender, age, race, nationality. Personal ambition, status, and moral codes enter into the act. We're defensive with somebody who's known as a tough bird and act cocksure with a pushover. All the while, other people are reacting to our personalities. It's all very complex; Dr. Jung barely scratched the surface. We can't change the psychology of behavior, but there is one thing that will make the difference in giving you the edge in the here and now: skill in negotiating. That is the one element you can and must control if you want the winner's chips to be on your side of the table.

Levin's Law: *No matter who you are or who you are fighting with, once you know the tactics of controlling an argument you can get the best of any deal.*

Any Number Can Play

If you want to go crazy with mathematical and theoretical bargaining possibilities, consider the matter of numbers. Different types of disputes involve different numbers of disputants, which can mean you're crossing swords with any number of assorted personalities. There is the one-to-one confrontation: you and me, nose to nose. Skirmishes in other trenches pit man against the organization, as in John Doe trying to outargue an IRS agent who's fronting for the entire Establishment. Other jousts match two on two, two on three, and so on through the numerical alphabet. In my profession, where most conflicts have to do with collective bargaining, the opponents are sometimes an individual union bargaining agent versus a management representative. More often, I'm sitting in with teams: groups of from four to ten people representing each side. The point is, whether your fight is one on one or team on team, it's not the numbers that count so much as it is your expertise in getting what it is you want and are entitled to.

By expertise I mean bargaining techniques. But before you can use them, you have to know what kind of conflict you're getting into, so you can choose the appropriate weapons. In short, if you're going to make the best of a fight, you have to know what the fight is all about. Just as the knowledgeable goalie skates into a hockey rink wearing leg protectors and not tennis shorts, the skillful negotiator is able to spot the kind of conflict and nature of his opponent's tactics, and goes in with the right ammunition.

The Three Basic Conflicts

The Manageable Conflict: Type A

Any dispute where you have the power to reach a satisfactory settlement of your differences is a manageable conflict. Spotting one is easy: If the other person has the authority to say yes, no, or give you what you want, then you're in a manageable situation. Your goal is reachable. If it's not, what you're in is an exercise in futility.

You may not realize it, but you have Type A problems all the time. It's a Type A when you argue with a policeman who insists on giving you a ticket. The cop has the authority to ticket you or not, and you have the power to talk him out of it. You're dealing in Type A when a car dealer or repairman quotes a price that's too high. He has the authority to come down or not, and you have the power to negotiate a deal—or walk out.

A Type A conflict is open to whatever strategies and tactics you can apply to change what the other person does. You can walk out, you can wheedle something extra into the deal, you can bargain for what you want and stand a good chance of getting it—if you know how to come up with a good argument.

Levin's Law: *The first offer is never the final offer.*

Use the right tactics and you'll shape the outcome your way. That's why it is important to be able to recognize a Type A situation. You start off with the attitude that you know you can be in the driver's seat by using any rational tactic at your command. The most important reminder you must constantly give yourself is that there is no good reason in the world why *you* should not be in charge.

The Veiled Conflict: Type B
A squabble where people are talking about one thing and really mean something else cannot be resolved. It's a charade, a phony, a game only a

patsy would walk into. You have to strip off the veils. Then you can win.

Where Do You Find Veils? All over. In domestic scenes, business, world affairs, between friends and passersby.

A woman I know, Barbara, is one of those people who's very involved in community work and proud of what she does. She is equally proud of her husband and his achievements, and is upfront about it. Paul, however, spends most of his time on his business. He rarely pays attention to her and Barbara's pride can't take it. She can't stand being ignored and is too proud to talk about it. So she argues with Paul about her clothing allowance instead. At least that gets a conversation rolling. Every week it's the same: She gets his attention, they battle, Paul hands her money—and walks out. This has been going on for years and a closetful of sables wouldn't solve the real problem. What Barbara is doing is trying to get compensated for her misery. Demanding more and more money is her way of getting paid for the attention she lacks.

I've seen the same kind of thing happen in factories, when workers are dissatisfied about conditions. They'll raise great storms over getting a raise, when what's basically bugging them is dirt and noise. The way they figure is, if they have to put up with rotten conditions, at least they should be paid for it.

What Do You Do with a Type B? Veiled conflicts are a pain. Since they are not valid in the first place, working with them takes doing.

Levin's Law: *The stated issue is not always the real issue.*

Bare the issue. Barbara should have realized that something was wrong when arguments just led to more arguments and didn't make her life better. She should have tackled her problem head on. The first step is to face the facts. If Barbara asked my advice, I'd encourage her to feel she deserves what she wants, and to be aboveboard in asking for it. I'd tell her to start by writing down on paper her real goal: "I want Paul to pay attention to me. I'm hurt because he ignores me." Writing it would force Barbara to be definite. Then I'd say, "Lay it on the line with Paul. Be direct. Tell him you're proud of him and want to please him, and you want him to show regard for you, too. Get your troubles out of the closet. And before you confront Paul, rehearse what you're going to say out loud once or twice. That will help you feel more confident and it will help break the rotten habit you've fallen into of always talking about something else."

Levin's Law: *To get real answers you must confront real questions.*

You have to stop hiding behind phony gripes if you want to make changes. Otherwise you will veil yourself into oblivion.

Change it into a manageable Type A. Paul should have suspected he was dealing with a veiled issue when Barbara was still dissatisfied no matter how much money he gave her for clothes. Walking away from the fights didn't help either. There's always a next meeting, and resentment grows when a conflict is not resolved.

I said to Paul, "This time why don't you try to settle your differences once and for all. Go back and find out what's behind Barbara's nagging. Be more patient, and be shrewd." That sounded good to him, so I spelled it out. I told him to play the baiting game. Toss out trial balloons to see what she grabs for. Test her with, "What if I gave you a trip to Mexico. Would that make you happy?" And not to worry about springing for the trip if she says yes. He could always back off with, "I just wanted to know how you felt about it."

You have to keep testing veiled issues until you hit the nerve. A change of scene can help find the sore spot, especially when the change means a relaxed, off-guard atmosphere. Smart businessmen use the technique when they want to find out what's really going on. They take customers, clients, associates to a restaurant or their health club and get them to loosen up. People can work up a pretty good talking jag over drinks and dinner, or lolling in the sauna. You need to do a little stroking and a lot of heavy listening, but that's a small price to pay for turning a veiled issue into a problem you can solve.

If you don't work on people to find out what's bugging them, you will go on floundering and wasting your time. Learn to tackle people's problems systematically, and stop fooling around. In the end, you'll come out happier and so will they.

Call in an outsider. Barbara or Paul could have gone to a psychologist, a marriage counselor, or some other consultant to work on surfacing their problem. While this isn't a bad idea, it isn't the greatest method in the world either. In any case, it beats playing amateur psychologist—a sure way to wind up in deep mire.

The Insoluble Conflict: Type C
There is almost no way you can deal with Type C conflicts. Period. They are drummed up purely for

the sake of causing rhubarbs and have little to do with resolving immediate, manageable problems.

What Do They Mean? Type C's are conflicts used to spotlight fervent causes, often political, and are fomented by people intent on grand change.

What to Do with an Insoluble. If you are picked as the tool or target, don't let yourself be roped in. You'll only get hurt. It simply isn't within your power to deliver what the revolutionists are shouting for. The best you can get is steamrollered. Or else weakened to the point of self-destruct.

Levin's Law: *Never let yourself be sucked in by people who are just trying to use you.*

Sometimes you can't escape, as university heads couldn't run from student demonstrators in the sixties. If you were a campus official and got stuck with having to quell a group of protestors, I'd tell you to splinter their big insoluble issue into small manageable ones that you could deal with one by one. Usually a group isn't solidly behind its leader anyway, so you could work on one segment's interest in nuclear research on campus, another's in feminism or late curfews, and so on. The tactic would split up the issue, and split up the group, too. Then you could whittle away at the smaller, more realistic complaints.

They will complain that you are trying to split them up and they will be right. Split them up anyway.

Levin's Law: *A group is the sum of separate elements. To weaken group strength, work on the parts, not the whole.*

The People You Meet in a Fight

People who argue are . . . people. It takes all kinds, as they say. What's interesting, in argument, is the characteristics with which you have to cope. Identifying them can tell you what stance will save your neck.

The Parent
The attitude is superior: "You can trust me. I'll never let you down. It's all in my hands. You don't have to worry about a thing. Just let me take care of it."

Don't let the parent put you down. He's playing the big adult; you play superadult: "All I want, sir, is what's coming to me. It will be better if we settle this matter jointly." He'll act hurt, as if you're the ingrate child. Don't let him snow you. He doesn't know what is best for you; you do. Handle him with, "I appreciate your concern, and that may be how you've dealt with this kind of problem before. But here's how it's going to be done now."

Remember Levin's Law that you don't have to take the first offer you hear. It's never the final one.

Blarneyer
He thinks flattery will get him everywhere. He tries to sweeten the pot by oozing compliments: "You're so intelligent, so quick, such an attractive person." Don't be sucked in; that's playing right into his oily hands. Shove the compliments aside with, "That's all well and good. Now let's talk about the issue." Or you can out-unctuous him, tongue in cheek: "Oh, but you are far more intelligent, quick, and attractive than anybody, and you're popular at dances besides." That should stop the silliness and move the discussion along.

Egomaniac

The Egomaniac comes on strong. But he's so intent on himself he only hears what's going on in his own head, not what you're saying. That's tough to deal with. Your best bet is to say matter-of-factly, "Come on, Joe, I know all the wonderful things you've done. What are you going to do for me today?" If that doesn't deflate him, do an end run. Find somebody who can overrule or influence him, so you can get your message across. If you do get him to listen to you, use his ego for your own gain. Plant your ideas so he'll think they're his: "As you said a while back, it would be a good idea to do thus-and-so." He'll crow about how smart he is, as he goes along with what you want.

Debater

This silver tongue carries on very convincingly, pouring out conclusions based on false premises. He will invent any fact that serves his ends: "Surveys show that 89.3 percent of all Chevrolets are purchased by women. Therefore you should advertise your cars in this women's publication." All you have to do is look for the specious core, strip it bare, and get down to basics.

Another good way to get the Debater where you can deal with him is to give him the Pavlov treatment. Inspect your nails, examine your watch, doodle industriously when he builds castles; pay rapt attention when he talks sense. He's not stupid. He'll learn in a hurry what turns you on.

Martinet

He's like your old gym teacher: loves straight lines and unswerving discipline. Goes by the book. He is rigid and narrow, has no imagination. You can't beat him by referring to the book because he's memorized every page. But you can try outbooking him by interpreting the regulations differently. Or convince him that the book doesn't apply.

Revolutionary

This is the archetypical Type C combatant. He and you are not dealing with the same issues. It's pointless to argue with him. Remember, he is just trying to use you. Don't let him. You might find an intermediary who can deal with him and redirect his gripe so it's something you can grapple with. He's playing to the grandstand, so you can try to win over his followers. Or you can walk out on him. Just don't give him an opening to complain that you refused to talk. If you walk, make sure the rest of the world knows why. A fourth alternative is to be more radical than the Revolutionary, and make him look like a conservative. Never let anybody get to your left.

Pugilist

There's always a chip on the belligerent's shoulder. He's cruising for trouble. Growls and roars a lot. Knock the chip off and chances are he'll back off You can take an equally bellicose stance and shout back. If that doesn't work, put on your coat and say you'll walk out if he doesn't talk calmly; you're not there to be yelled at. Once you get leverage on the situation stay on top. Put the pressure on, and make him face up to you and the issue. Look for the Pugilist's glass jaw. His weakness is your strength—if you use it.

Victim

"I had nothing to do with what happened. I didn't know what was going on. It's Joe's fault. You're hurting my feelings, accusing me." The victim tries to weasel out by lying, by crying, by deflecting you from the real problem. It's such transparent baloney, all you have to do is call him on it and make him get down to business.

Charmer
A delightful companion and conversationalist. Tries to control you by putting you at ease. Relax and enjoy it. He's easy to deal with, as long as you make sure you stick to the issue at hand and don't let him charm you out of what you want. You might as well go with the flow and charm back. It's fun. Besides, you catch more flies with honey than with vinegar.

The Nice Person
The Nice Person is a rat. He gets you by coming on as the consummate well-bred gentleman. He waves his important, well-bred contacts under your nose. Harps on how important it is to be ethical. He forces you to return civility with civility, and all the while he is murdering you. Your only weapon against the Nice Person is to be more sanctimonious than he is, while you fight back relentlessly.

Never let a Nice Person make you feel guilty about your anger. He deserves it.

Sex Fiend
He or she may or may not crave your body: What he or she wants is to screw you by . . . all right, by screwing you. If you feel like having an affair and can handle it, go ahead. But be aware that the hurly-burly you enjoy in the bedroom can haunt you when you're talking business in the boardroom.

Steel Trap

The deadliest enemy of all. The Steel Trap is cold, calculating, nerveless. He knows who is guilty and who is innocent. He is determined to wreak justice —his way. The Steel Trap is hard to budge because his mind is made up and he doesn't want to talk it over. Even bargaining as hard as you can, you may go under. You have to keep reminding yourself that conflict is opportunity. You can get him from behind the scenes. Do an end run. Get word to his superiors that he's unreasonable and obstructive. Have somebody else deal with him for you. Make allies of other people he's killed and build up the pressure of ill will so he'll have to retrench. Or show him you're onto his game. Mirror his steel-trap style and force him to be manageable. Or else—get him the next time.

You Have to Make Them Like You; You're Going to Meet Them Again

Whether you win or whether you lose, you're going to see the same character or his counterpart again. That's how life is. People constantly climb up and down the same ladder you're on. If they like you, they'll give you a hand. If you've clobbered them, watch out. You're apt to get clobbered back.

You have to understand that every time you get into a disagreement it's going to end with one of you winning and one of you losing, or else in a draw. And you're probably going to meet the same people you beat in other disagreements. Most of us have our battles over and over again with the same people. How they feel about you depends on how skillfully you managed the last fight. So you have to think ahead. What is it you might want from them in the future? Will it matter to you if they hate you and want revenge? If not, go ahead and lunge for the groin. Get your win any way you can. Be a kamikaze. But remember, it's suicide unless you're sure you'll never need those people again.

If you're not sure, stop and think before you plunge ahead. Figure out what the upshot of your behavior can be. If you get what you want out of the disagreement, what will they get—hard feelings, or will they like you anyway? You can make people give you what you want and feel good about it if you learn the difference between kamikaze and skillful maneuvering. I'm going to teach you the system, just as I've taught it to others.

The Art of Winning
There's a fellow named Frank who lives on the second floor in my building; we often stop to talk in the lobby. He's an attorney, not quite as successful as some of the partners in his firm. He worries about that and he worries about his relationships in the courtroom. He's never sure if he's done the right thing. Often when he wins a case he feels guilty because he's barbecued his opponent. I tell Frank he doesn't understand the difference between kamikaze-tough and skillful-tough.

Kamikaze is when you barrel through to an all-out win. It's when winning can be losing.

I can't remember a time at the bargaining table, the courtroom, or in private life when an all-out win has been the best outcome of an argument. Where there's a heavy winner, there has to be a heavy loser —waiting his turn to get even. Some time, some way, that loser is going to be in a position to reclaim his losses, repossess his turf, restore his damaged image. Heavy winner beware; a loser will get you when he can.

"Skillful," I tell Frank, is knowing how to maneuver the other guy into winning, too. It's a system that sets up a mutual exchange of advantages. You stand up for what you want and win it, but you set up the other guy so he gets what he wants, too. Set him up—because you're going to meet him again. The next time around, you want him to feel that things will come out OK, with you to deal with. You want him to trust you and cooperate.

The Art of Triumph
Some days Frank wins and feels good about himself. We talk about that, too. He grins when I tell him he's a master of the fine art of winning nice. The big thing about winning is, *never rub anybody's nose in your win*. It's rotten to gloat over anybody's wounded sensibilities.

There's also a practical reason for winning nice. Wise winners show mercy and understanding if for no better reason than not to antagonize people into revenge. They always make sure losers feel decent, so they'll be friends in the next encounter.

Frank has an innate concern for other people's feelings. I like how he soothes their egos. Some of his favorite phrases should go into your peace-making repertoire. If they work on lawyers, they'll probably work on most people.

Next time around you'll probably wind up holding the cards.
You did a great job. I guess this just wasn't your turn.
It's been a real pleasure for me to deal with a pro like you.
You win some, you lose some.

You Can Learn a Lot from a Loss

Some mornings I see Frank and it's plain he's had a bad night. He says he's had them for years. Finds himself talking to the ceiling all night after a drubbing, replaying the day's battle and thinking, I should have said this, why didn't I do that? I tell Frank he needs to use his energy in constructive analysis. "Think of loss as opportunity. Use those sleepless nights to review what went well and critique what you did wrong. The next time you'll be able to identify and use winning strategies faster."

I guarantee you Frank's successful partners aren't talking to the ceilings nights. They're strategizing for the next day's win.

The artful loser examines every defeat for some element he can take advantage of. He doesn't feel guilty about losing, or say, "There's nothing more I can do." You've heard about snatching victory from the jaws of defeat? This is it. When you fight with the plumber and he ends up overcharging you anyway, it's your chance to find a better plumber next time the pipes go haywire. When an administrative manager with IBM told me he'd lost out on the transfer to Dallas that he'd been angling for and was assigned to a marketing job in Topeka instead, I told him to quit groaning and carrying on like a failure. This was his chance to learn a new field and add to his credentials, to meet people he could use later on, and to lay the groundwork for another step up the ladder.

Levin's Law: *Keep thinking of how you can win more the next time.*

Never Take a Loss Personally
On bad days when I see Frank in the lobby, I can
tell he's lost a case. He looks defeated. I'm sure his
wife feels it, too. The problem is, he doesn't understand that a fight is nothing more than the sum total
of objective forces at work: issues, strategies, tactics,
and incidental circumstances. Sometimes you win,
often you lose; there'll always be a next time. The
key point is, losing is nothing to get emotional about.
Levin's Law: *Never take a loss personally.*

What happened to you would have happened
to anyone in your position. This one was a loss. From
here on, be smart enough to change the proportion
of wins and losses so the balance is in your favor.

Some Losers Never Learn
Frank is an occasional loser and that's OK; you can
make deals with him.
I hate born losers. They're a problem for everyone. Stupid. Inept. Or else playing a game to get
sympathy as an underdog. Born losers are tough to
do business with. They dart after rainbows they
can't possibly have. They complicate things, brew
trouble over trivia, wander down sidetracks, listen
to nobody, miss the point, let ripe moments slip away
into oblivion. What can you do with a born loser?
You can do several things, though perhaps with
no great joy. For one thing, you can be kind. You
might as well; a loser is like an animal addicted to
showing its jugular. Being savage with him won't
accomplish a thing. With more difficulty, you can
carry the loser. Make the decisions for him, lead

him, cover so he won't look bad, fashion solutions he can cope with in spite of himself.

A more useful step is to work around him. Deal behind the scenes with somebody who has the power and authority to make a deal. This is known as the end run, and the faster you run the better. Even if a loser is, temporarily, the head of his organization, he'll foul things up for you. His only future is to ruin the business or be replaced by somebody who can handle it.

By whatever means at hand, it is charity all around to stay clear of congenital losers. They're sure to pull you down with them. Avoid all temptation to let them cling and enfold you in their failures. They are disarming in their ability to make you feel sorry for them. So were the little foxes—up to a point.

Measuring Wins and Losses

One of the things that always perplexes Frank is how he stands when he wins a case. He's afraid if the judgment is heavily in his favor, the other lawyer will try to kill him next time they're face-to-face in a courtroom. He's probably right.

One evening I ran into Frank and he looked so triumphant it would have been comical if I didn't know how seriously he takes things. He'd just wound up an accident case where his client got $225,000 in an arrangement that gave the defendant five years to pay it, with interest. I said, "That's great, Frank. Congratulations. That win is going to help your career a lot." He thanked me and raced off to share the good news with his wife. The next morning he had that worried look again; I guessed what was on his mind. I took him aside and told him he'd gotten more of a win than he realized. His agreement to let the defendant take five years to pay out the verdict meant the other lawyer had won something too: His client didn't have to part with all that capital at once. "Wait and see," I said. "That lawyer's going to be delighted to deal with you next time you oppose him. You did a good job getting a deal that works two ways."

The disputes you have every day can come out in a hundred different ways ranging from rotten to wonderful, depending on where you stand. The best resolution is when you're satisfied with what you got and so is the other guy. The worst is when you both take a licking. You have to recognize what the gradations mean, so you can see what kind of solution to aim for: what its effects will be on the people you fight with—again and again.

Part of the system of winning well is to measure results in terms of satisfaction, or acceptability. It doesn't matter whether your bout is in a courtroom or in business, if it's a personal war or a global contest. The measurements are the same. So you can understand what they mean, I've devised a way to visualize good, bad, and mediocre outcomes. I call it the Conflict Grid.

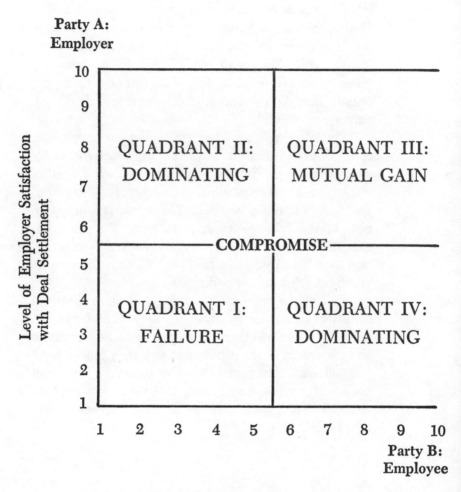

Party A:
Employer

Level of Employer Satisfaction with Deal Settlement

10

9

8 QUADRANT II: QUADRANT III:
7 DOMINATING MUTUAL GAIN

6 ————COMPROMISE————

5

4 QUADRANT I: QUADRANT IV:
3 FAILURE DOMINATING

2

1

1 2 3 4 5 6 7 8 9 10

Party B:
Employee

Level of Employee Satisfaction
with Deal Settlement

The Levin Conflict Grid

In this visualization of a dispute over wages, the vertical line (Party A) represents the boss and the horizontal line (Party B) represents the employee. The numbers along each line represent the level of satisfaction each of the parties attaches to the resolution of the conflict.

1-1. If both parties are dissatisfied with the outcome, their degrees of acceptability will intersect at the lowest possible point: 1-1 in the Failure quadrant.

10-1. If the employee gets the full wage increase he asks for, his acceptability factor will be high: 10. If at the same time the boss feels he took a beating and is paying out too much money, his acceptability factor will be low: 1. The resulting 1-10 is in the Dominating quadrant.

If the company succeeds in reducing the employee's wages, so the employee believes he has lost everything and gained nothing, the 10-1 ratio will be switched to 1-10, and remain in one of the two Dominating quadrants.

10-10. If the employee wins his raise and company profits climb due to his productivity, the result will be a mutually satisfying 10-10 degree of acceptability. This is the ultimate, a full Mutual Gain solution.

5-5. If both parties compromise, with neither of them gaining nor losing everything, their acceptabilities will intersect in the center of the Conflict Grid, at the 5-5 Compromise point.

All other degrees of acceptability fall within one of the four quadrants as indicated in the diagram.

The Meaning of Acceptability

Your view of acceptability may be your opponent's idea of poison; it depends on what you each hoped for and what the results are worth to you. On the preceding conflict grid, the employee may have asked for a $60-a-week raise, tacitly expecting $40 at the most. If he got $40, he'd have felt this was a terrific gain and would peg his degree of acceptability at a full 10. That same $40-a-week raise might be viewed by the company as a 10 for them and a 7 for the employee. They'd feel the employee hadn't gotten everything he'd asked for but that they'd given him enough so they'd get good work and good will from him. In other words, acceptability isn't necessarily based on numbers; it's in the eye of the bargainer.

The Quadrants of Acceptability

Quadrant I: Failure

This is the quadrant of joint despair. Learn to see it coming so you can switch tactics and not land in it. Failure is when you and your rival both believe you have taken a loss. This is what happened after the 1966 and 1967 New York City newspaper strikes, when the typographers' union walked out on the papers. When the smoke cleared, the union had gotten its pay hike, but there was no more *World Journal Tribune*. Or *Herald Tribune*. Or *World Telegram and Sun*. The newspapers were out of business. The workers had their raises, but no jobs. Both sides lost.

You can see examples everywhere. The Failure quadrant is the final resting place when you can't resolve your differences with your husband or wife and end up in a nasty divorce. It's where you and another guy knock each other out fighting for the same promotion, only to have an outsider hired for the job. The two of you skulk back to your desks, glaring at each other.

In Quadrant I resolutions, you and your opponent walk away badly bloodied without having gained any advantage. What's left between you is mutual distrust, fear, frustration, and hostility—motivations enough for further bloody battles. Whenever anybody comes to me with this problem, I tell him the relationship can be put back on a trusting, productive footing, but it's going to take a lot of work and a lot of time. You have to go step by step, admitting to the other person you were wrong to let the relationship suffer . . . what happened was regrettable . . . you want to close the door on bygones. You have to begin to reestablish confidence by offering your help and following through on every offer: "I'll have Joe call you tomorrow. . . . I'll look up the information and get right back to you. . . ." You're as cooperative as honeymooners on the wedding night, slowly rebuilding the trust you've blown.

Quadrants II and IV: Dominating

In Quadrants II and IV one of you is elated with the solution and the other finds it a total bust. This often happens when you're poorly matched in skill and bargaining power. I remember a strike called by a teachers' union against a school district. The teachers wanted a salary increase; the school board not only fought the increase, but also collected legal fines from the union for as long as the teachers were on strike. With no strong incentive to settle the dispute unless the teachers went back to work at their old salaries, the school board was in a position to hold out against union demands for a very long time. They did. Finally convinced of the board's ability to outwait them, the teachers went back to their jobs—minus a salary increase, and with losses in both pay and self-image. The board, on the other hand, was in its glory. It saved the money it would have had to pay in increases, raked in union fines during the strike, and piled up political mileage by showing it could be tough on labor. The glory didn't last long; what they didn't count on was the cost in good will. The teachers went back to work seething with resentment and plotting retaliation. They were determined to get even however they could.

Quadrant III: Mutual Gain
When you and your opponent both think your disagreement wound up wonderfully, it's because you both got more than you were after. The way to achieve this is to learn to decide what you want before you lunge ahead, analyze the situation, and maneuver the other person so he wins as much as you. The final fillip is to make the situation yield benefits you hadn't expected. It can be done.

I have a friend who's an ad salesman. Very high-powered. Antsy. Wants to get everything done yesterday and never has time to talk—except to a prospect. Dick and I were having a drink one day and he told me he'd been scuffling with one of the other salesmen, Joe, over an office problem that was driving him nuts. He was fed up. It looked like a no-win to him and if he couldn't do something about that jackass Joe . . .

The story was, Dick shared a secretary with Joe and the two were constantly at each other's neck about using her to get out their weekly call reports.

Dick insisted, rightly, on giving his dictation at the end of every Friday morning. So did Joe. Of course it wasn't working; Dick was in a purple fury just telling me about it. I told him, "You want what you want and there's no reason you can't have it." I outlined what he could do. I told him to look at the situation as a problem in simple logistics, and to talk with Joe about solving it. Get his cooperation. Give him an idea. I urged Dick to try this one on for size: "Let Joe give his Friday dictation to the secretary while you give yours to a machine for transcription. You can take turns; alternate weeks you use the secretary while Joe feeds into the machine." The idea worked—and better than they had expected. Not only did they both get their reports out on time and without hassles, but the machine let them take care of extra correspondence and memos.

The lesson from what I taught Dick is this: There are plenty of ways you can skin a cat. The best is to think up an idea so everyone wins.

Levin's Law: *Everyone should win something.*

In the Middle: Compromise
A compromise is something both you and your opponent can live with. It's as simple as that. You compromise every time you resolve a situation so that nobody's hurt. Maybe it's nothing to write home to mother about, but at least you're equally satisfied or dissatisfied with the answer. And—very important —neither of you has reason to hate the other.

People can work up a lot of hate when the problem is divorce. Money's at stake. Children. Pride. It's the soap opera of all time. A divorcing couple I know, Mike and Donna, came to me when they started battling over their six-year-old. Rather, Mike came to me. Donna was busy running around telling her friends what an unreasonable monster he was, how she's supposed to have full custody and there he is demanding he come visit anytime he wants to. She'd never have any privacy and the child wouldn't know which end was up. You know the scene. As Mike told it to me, it was clear the only thing he and Donna agreed on was that the arrangement would be rotten for them both. I said, "Mike, sit down and talk with Donna about it. You don't want her so mad at you she'll turn the child against you out of spite. And she doesn't want you to come barging around on her time. Try to find a way you can manage this thing conveniently."

Mike followed up. He and Donna worked the problem through and solved their differences without bloodshed. He takes the child during summer vacations and every other weekend, and Donna has custody the rest of the time. She has the control she's looking for, and Mike knows exactly when he can be with his child.

You have to learn to create compromise solutions so you can get what you want in life and not leave a trail of enemies out to get you.

The Best Quadrant of All and How to Get There

It's obvious that the most desirable of all positions on the Conflict Grid is in a Mutual Gain quadrant. It is also the most difficult to arrive at. The one basic element you need is mutual trust, a quality that is not built overnight. You have to put a lot of time and effort into getting somebody to trust you. At that, the trust you've carefully built can be swept out from under you by a heedless wrong move. Especially in a disagreement. After all, the reason you're at odds with somebody in the first place is because you don't trust each other's ideas about goals.

Put yourself in this scene as one of the people who were involved in a classic study on trust, and you'll see the effects it has on winning and losing.

The Bell Jar Grapple
In the first part of this rather whacky experiment six people were positioned around a bell jar that contained six Ping-Pong balls the exact size of the neck of the jar. Each ball had a string attached to it and each participant was handed a string. They were told that the object of the game was to be the first person to tug his ball out of the jar. All six players immediately pulled on their strings at once, bent on being first. The result was, all six Ping-Pong balls jammed together in the neck of the bottle. Nobody won.

Then a second group of six was told that the object of the game was simply to pull all the balls out of the jar. Any order would do. This time, the players got together and strategized. Each would cooperate with the other and pull on his ball in turn. Presto, they emptied the jar and everybody won.

The lesson is clear. When you go for winner-take-all by getting ahead on your own, nobody wins. You have to make people trust and work with you to get what you want. That is pure Mutual Gain.

Panic in the Bell Jar, Crisis in Conflict
When everybody's pulling for his own good and all the balls are stuck, you have a crisis on your hands. Progress stops dead in its tracks. Nobody can move and nobody can win. Everyone's on the ropes, tense and frustrated.

The good news is, that's the breaking point.

People crave anything that will get rid of the agony of their frustration. So much, they'll listen to any decent proposal you come up with. Crisis is your big chance.

Rethink what you are doing. What is the object of the game? What do you really want? What's another way to get it? A fresh point of view can bring the answer. Change your thinking from "I'm going to be the winner" to "There has to be some collective solution" and you can open doors to new and profitable ideas.

Crisis Is Opportunity

Most people think of crisis as danger. They try to avoid it. They see only their own frustration and miss the point: *Crisis is a vehicle, not an obstacle.* Miss the moment when you can leap in with a reasonable way to get frustration and anger off the other person's back, and the best that will happen is your opponent will break off the discussion just to end his misery. You have to come up with ways to relieve the frustration and lay groundwork for a solution.

A 2 A.M. phone call from Los Angeles not long ago brought crisis to my bedside. I wasn't surprised to hear Jack's voice. He'd wake up anybody at any hour if it served his purpose; consideration is not his middle name. Jack is a television producer I met on the coast. He's a cocky, flashy type, impressed with himself. I already knew that he'd been having a red-hot affair with an actress and was neglecting his family in the process. Now he was having a battle royal with his wife and the fight had reached the crisis stage. That's why he called. Marge had found out about Jack's philandering and it was the last straw. Or so she said. She told him she was through. She'd suspected for a long time that he was fooling around. There were plenty of other things she couldn't stand about him besides. This was it. Jack described his end of the quarrel to me. He said he'd gotten plenty of gripes off his chest. Told Marge she was snobby and aloof, acted as if Hollywood weren't good enough for her. Marge swung back with how he'd always been inconsiderate of her. They both hit the high notes and Jack was in a panic when he called. They were ready to call it quits but couldn't even come to terms on that. He wanted to know what I thought.

I said, "Look, Jack, you can split up and that will get you off the crisis. But I bet it'll cost you a fortune if you go through with a divorce. Marge will be miserable and so will the kids. She doesn't want a divorce. She wants better working conditions. Tell me the truth, don't you really want to save this marriage? Isn't that why you're upset?" He agreed that that was so and asked what the hell he could do. I said, "I can't tell you how to save your marriage, Jack, but I can tell you how to arrive at some kind of an agreement with Marge. And I can tell you this: If you don't pursue it now, you're crazy. This is an opportunity you may never have again."

Jack broke in. "Are you kidding? After what I just described?"

"That's right. She'll be relieved that you came back. It's a sign to her that you care. Sit down with her and without getting into a shouting match, try to identify all the problems. Is it where you live? Is it your dirty socks? Is it that you keep late hours? And are you bugged because she's aloof? Because she doesn't appear to understand your work? Because she spends too much money? Can you both find someplace to give a little? Make a list of the complaints on both sides of the picture. Lay it all out."

Levin's Law: *You have got to understand what it is your opponent wants and what you are willing to give. Otherwise you will just have a stalemate.*

Learn to bargain every day. At least that way there's a chance.

If you have a system and know what you are doing, nobody can get the better of you.

Three

The Language of Conflict

Speech is a faculty given to man to conceal his thoughts.

—TALLEYRAND

*T*HE SAME THING happens in bargaining that happens in travel. If you don't know the local language, you're stymied. You have to be able to make your needs known and understand what people are telling you, if you want to hold your own in foreign territory.

Essential as it is to learn to speak bargainese, listening right can save your life. If you miss out on deals and never know why, it may be that you're so intent on what's going on in your own head, you are not listening thoroughly. Bargaining is a two-way street. You have to stay tuned in to every smoke signal and clue that comes from the other person. And you have to know what to listen for. What you hear isn't always what's being said.

Tiny Words Have Mighty Meanings

Pay attention. A single word can change the course of an argument. Miss it and you'll lose your way. Your sparring partner changes "I'll never give you what you want" to "I don't believe I can give you what you want." The change in language is your chance. Take it. Now that you know he isn't sure of where he stands, close in and convince him to swing things your way.

Testing, 1, 2 . . .
Learn to listen for the sound of balloons being tested to see if they fly. They give off messages in the form of low-pitched whirrs. They are money in the bank when you hear them.

Alec is a free-lance photographer. Not a top-notcher, but a good, conscientious craftsman. Even though he gets a lot of work, he struggles to make ends met. It makes him furious. He says he's never gotten a good deal in his life: The world is out to rip him off. "They get away with it because I'm an artist, not a businessman. They take advantage of me and I practically lose money on every job I get. Just once I'd like to outsmart a client and get what's coming to me." The way Alec operates I'm not surprised he's in trouble. He is dedicated to his camera and mindless when it comes to anything else. Some editor will say, "I need a couple of shots to illustrate this article. It's about one thousand dollars of work. Think you can handle it?" Alec hears "one thousand dollars" and misses the bargaining word, *about*. Then he goes out and kills himself to do a good job, turns in a $1,500 effort, and submits his bill for $1,000. He thinks he's stuck with what he heard the editor say. He never fails to complain. "That cheapskate. He's like all the rest. I should have known I'd be taken for a ride."

I told Alec he'll keep on being taken if he doesn't learn to listen better. People aren't necessarily cheap; they just want the best deal they can wangle. When that editor said "about one thousand dollars," he was telling Alec that the door was open for negotiation. Alec let the door slam on his nose.

You have to learn to listen for the possibilities in a deal. When somebody tests you, make the most of it. They're waiting for you to make an offer and get the bargaining going. My advice is, start out high, and don't settle for less than you deserve.

Slips of the Lip

Verbal lapses are revealing. They're mirrors of the mind, and you may be the one who's making them.

My secretary, Betty, is one of those people who always feels everybody walks all over her: She's always the one who has to give in on a situation. She tells a story on herself that happened when she was working in another office.

She and two other secretaries were scheduling their two-week vacations for the year. It worked out that one of the three would have to split her two weeks so that the office would be covered full time. Naturally, each of them wanted two consecutive weeks so they could travel, and they must have spent a month wrangling over who'd be stuck with the split vacation. One morning as they were chattering, Betty said, "It might be fun to try one of those singles ski places for a week in February."

I pointed out to her, "Do you understand that what you said gave those two people a message— that you would be willing to take the split vacation? If the other two secretaries were clever, they'd have picked you up on it." Sure enough, they had. Betty says that from now on she's going to watch what she says.

Unlike Betty's co-workers, most listeners are too polite or preoccupied to pick up on the truth hung naked. They careen ahead, tires screeching, just as if they'd heard what they'd expected to hear and the ripe moment passes, unplucked. Nobody notices because the speaker hasn't heard his own lapse either.

He'd be astonished if he were called on it. "Did I say that?"

Then there's the risible slip. I hope some labor historian records the time a screw manufacturing company laid off half its employees and the news headline was EIGHTY WOMEN LAID BY AMERICAN SCREW. Mirror of the reporter's mind, and a pretty accurate headline at that.

Verbal Swordplay

There are threats and there are bluffs. If you listen well, you can tell which is which. A real threat is thoroughly credible, backed by the power and intent to follow through. A bluff is strategy intended to scare you. The words themselves aren't what counts, it's the strategy you have to recognize.

My mother was New York's master bluffer. When I was a kid she used to take me with her to do the family shopping on Orchard Street, the great haggling center of the world. Her method was to go into a store, dicker with the shopkeeper over the price, shake her head, and walk out. The shopkeeper would call her back in with an offer. She'd walk out again, he'd call her back in with another offer. This would go on any number of times until he stopped calling her in. That's when she'd turn around, go back into the store, and buy the merchandise at his last price. But not without taking a last stab at shaving off a couple of more cents. She knew she was bluffing, but she was so good at it the shopkeeper could never be sure.

Bluffers don't really intend to deliver on their threats. Kids know this. If they're told once they're told a thousand times to pick up their toys or go without supper. I've never seen a hungry kid. The trouble with that kind of bluff is, if the parent ever tries a genuine threat, the child will assume it's just another bluff and continue to do as he pleases.

Levin's Law: *The key to effective threats is believability.*

Imagine this scenario: A manufacturer and supplier are dickering over a business deal. They can't agree on the price. The manufacturer goes to the door and says, "I'm leaving right now if you don't meet my price."

Imagine the scene again. This time the manufacturer says, "I'd like to talk further but I have to leave." He waves a plane ticket as he goes to the door.

Notice the extra strategy in the credible threat. The manufacturer doesn't say, "I'm leaving forever." He's not cutting off his nose to spite his face. He leaves space in his walkout for the supplier to make him an offer, either on the spot or by calling back later.

Levin's Law: *Let them know you mean what you say, and make it possible for them to give you what you want.*

The Vocabulary of Latitude

When somebody talks in terms of leeway—"I need to earn two hundred fifty to three hundred dollars a week," "I'll give you a six to eight percent raise," "I'll pay eight to ten dollars for that"—don't take him literally. Listen to what he's really saying.

You are applying for a job. The employer asks how much salary you need. In innocence, you say $300 to $350 a week, not wanting to sound pushy but hoping to hear a generous, "Three-fifty it is." The employer, the person who's paying, hears the $300 to $350 differently. To him it's an opportunity to get good help at $300 a week.

Announcing leeway is a ritual of bargaining. It gives the illusion you can always move up or back down, even though the odds are against it. More important, you're telling them something. "I'll take three hundred to three hundred fifty dollars a week" means $350 is the most you think you can get.

Levin's Law: *There is an important message in every statement of leeway. Range is not leeway, it is a message.*

Off-the-Wall Answers

In my early professional days, I used to think there was something wrong with (a) my hearing, (b) my brain. People were forever saying things that had nothing to do with the question at hand. Eventually, I focused on the irrelevancies and could see that there's a pattern to them. Irrelevancies are a strategy people use to avoid giving definite answers.

My friend Bob was trying to sell his boat. He figured it was worth $50,000 and he had a buyer who was dying to own the boat. But the buyer said no, $50,000 was too much; he might pay $45,000. Out of nowhere Bob began talking about what a great time he had with the boat, how he loved sunning on the fantail and putting in at harbor islands for afternoon picnics. That boat was Bob's wife and mistress, to hear him tell it. The buyer began to get anxious; maybe he'd never get his hands on the boat. As soon as Bob saw the buyer squirm, he went back to the bargaining. "How about it? Fifty thousand and it's yours." The buyer just couldn't swing it;

$45,000 was his limit. Bob said, "I hate to sell her and I really want fifty thousand dollars, but to make it easier for you, I'll throw in some extra sails and a radiophone." That sounded like a good deal, and the buyer took the bait.

Bob had withheld the extras so he could throw them in if he had to. He'd launched into irrelevant comments about the joys of sunshine and island picnicking to test the buyer's interest. He had to find out what the buyer's no really meant, to see if he could get the price up that extra $5,000.

Some people shower you with off-the-wall talk to cover their uncertainty. How often have you heard someone in a tight spot start churning out sentences like fusillades of tap steps? The fancy footwork is supposed to addle you so you won't pursue the subject. And what they churn out is so vague they can make the words mean anything they want to later on. Slice through fast. Ask pointed questions and get at the facts. Remind yourself: It isn't your fault you can't understand what they're saying. You have to find out if they are confused, stalling, or setting you up.

You can't credit every opponent with being strategically shrewd. Confused statements are also the product of confused minds.

Levin's Law: *If you aren't straight in your head about what you want to say, it won't come out straight.*

Does No Mean Yes, or Does It Mean No?

There's an old gag that has the girl squealing, "No! Please, Johnny!" as the couple fades into the bedroom. The punch line is, "Which is it, 'No' or 'Please'?"

Levin's Law: *Never take an answer at face value.*

A yes or a no is as good or bad as you make it. Once you know that, you can listen to argumentative yesses and nos till the cows come home—and barrel through until you get the answer you want.

A no is not a no when it's not time to make a commitment. Bob didn't take his buyer's early no seriously. He kept right on bargaining until he'd gotten everything he could out of the deal. The buyer wasn't so dumb, either. If he'd given a fast yes, that would have sealed the bargain then and there. He'd never have gotten the radiophone thrown in.

A no is not a no when it's not justified. Bob knew his buyer's eagerness for the boat. He knew the buyer's budget. And he knew the price was right. Bob kept plugging until he made the sale.

A no is not a no when it's conditional. "No, but." "No, but I'll check it out with someone." "No, unless you do something for me." Listen for the language surrounding no. "No, but" means you can turn it into a yes.

What if the Answer Isn't Yes and It Isn't No?

You can pin down a vague or iffy answer if you hear it as a signal to push the other person over the line. Sometimes vagueness is just a stall: "Let's see what happens." (Parents use that one all the time on helpless children.) "I wouldn't give you a definite no on that" is practically handing you a positive yes, if you hear and use it right. It leaves the door open for discussion. "I don't know. Let's put it on the back

burner" is an invitation to bring up the subject
again when the time is right.

You have to constantly remind yourself of Levin's
Laws, and keep looking for new ways to solve your
problems.

It's the Way That You Say It

Tone, inflection, a shrug of the shoulders, or wink
of the eye has everything to do with the language of
conflict. You can win, lose, or change a fight just by
smiling. It takes the edge off a harsh statement. Or
you can scare the marrow out of someone with a
sinister Dan Duryea delivery.

For proof, try this experiment at your next cock-
tail party. Say "You are going to go to bed tonight
at eight o'clock" to three attractive strangers, in
three different ways: sternly, with amazement, with
sexual innuendo. People respond to tone—and I wish
you the best of luck at the party.

Tone and diction can underscore the importance
of a message. Loud and clear means the speaker
wants to be heard. Mumbling is for people who
want their messages muffled. Rapid muttering into
the chin means uncertainty, fear of attack, or a wish
that the whole thing were over with.

Pay attention to how people speak as well as to
what they say. And remember, the smart ones are
listening to you the same way.

Volume and tempo are useful reverse-English
devices. When everyone else is outshouting each
other hammer and tong, you can get their attention
with one even louder shout. In the hush that follows,
punctuate what you have to say by speaking in a
low, hard-to-hear, deliberately slow voice.

If your usual style is quiet and cool, turning up

the volume once in a blue moon can give a statement of fact the power of a cannon. It startles people into, "Wow! I've never seen you get angry. You must be terribly upset about this."

On the other hand, starched formality will devastate people you're angry or impatient with. "My dear sir" can be the ultimate sarcasm.

Never Throw Verbal Pie in Anybody's Face

The saintliest among us are tempted at times to speak insultingly to an opponent or colleague. The wisest among us refrain. The withering dig, the disdainful scoff, may feel like fun at the moment. It's bound to boomerang and explode in your face.

I once watched a school board destroy its own position because of an intrateam insult. I was mediating a bargaining session between the board and a teachers' union. While we were at the table, one of the board members came up with a suggestion for new salary guidelines. His chairman sneered, "That is the most stupid idea I've heard today. Any idiot could see it'd never work. Why don't you just be still and let me do the thinking around here?" The humiliated board member was so devastated by losing face in front of both teams, he gummed up his own team's works to get even. He took privy information about the amount the board had secretly decided it would be willing to pay the teachers, and leaked it to a union representative. The leak settled the board's hash. Once the teachers knew where they stood, the board had no clout.

Husbands and wives seem particularly prone to use insults to try to gain an advantage, though I don't know why I pick on married couples. The wobbly technique is just as common when neighbor

argues with neighbor, customer fights with trades-
person, or businessman fights with businessman.
They'll needle the adversary into smacking them,
verbally or physically, so they'll look benighted and
win sympathy. It rarely fails: The victims get even
by finding a weak spot and smacking back. Abuse
does not pay.

The Echo Effect

When people smile, you smile, and then they smile
back. When they snarl, you snarl, and so on. Keep
it up and your echoes of each other fuse into a
mostly smiling or snarling discussion.

I'm simplifying, for the sake of illustration, the
effect people have on each other in fights and other
everyday relationships. Each side's strong characteristics are adopted by the other and become the over-
all, permeating style. The echo effect is why when
a couple marries and one is violent, the pair becomes
known as "that violent couple." It's why groups such
as the Teamsters Union are rough-and-tough bunches:
The teamsters were spawned during Prohibition by
rough, tough rumrunners. Their style has echoed
through the decades.

In arguments, if one side is belligerent, the other
will drop its Mary Mild personality and become
belligerent, too. Threats breed threats, derision be-
gets derision; battles take on a characteristic over-
tone. Buzz words are picked up and bounced back
until they become the vocabulary of the argument.
Rivals begin dressing alike. Even one person's concept, when it's presented forcefully, becomes the
common accepted standard for both.

This chameleonlike phenomenon is a fact of
life. It will not harm you if you know how to use it.

Echoes are like rainbows and orgasms. You can't
plan or stop them, but you can understand why they
exist.

The Power of Holding Your Tongue

As persuasive as rhetoric can be, silence can be a
more potent and eloquent tactic. The language of
silence is essential in bargainese. You have to learn
when to be still, what silence does to other people,
what it can do for you.

If a soft answer turneth away wrath, no answer
can turn away trouble. Silence makes people babble.
They think they have to fill every void, as if they'd
be fined by the FCC for the sin of dead air. They
dig themselves into holes filled with nonsense, and
often prattle the secret thoughts on their mind or
information they shouldn't have leaked. You can
learn a lot if you keep still and let the other person
pour out the beans.

On the other hand, somebody else can stay silent
and learn your secrets by getting you to babble.
Don't fall for the trap. The defense against taciturn-
ity is to hold your tongue. Or else change the subject.
Let them dig their own grave, not yours.

I know a woman named Susan who was arguing
with a man in her office about a secretary they were
going to hire. She told me that her co-worker, Hal,
was absolutely determined to hire a woman who was
not qualified for the job. Susan was upset. She was
the one who'd have to work with the new woman.
She didn't know how to handle Hal and get rid of
the problem. Her first impulse was to argue with
him and turn on the hysterics. She realized that
would only make him more determined to defend
his choice and beef up the other woman's position.

I suggested she ask Hal to make a list of the woman's qualifications and tell Susan why she should be hired. Susan kept still, while he thrashed around searching for the nonexistent reasons and wound up sputtering a lot of nonsense. He talked his own candidate out of a job.

Levin's Law: *Whenever you can let someone dig his own grave, let him. He'll do a better job than you will.*

Silent Language

You can tell somebody that you are stubborn, aggressive, defensive, or agreeable without ever opening your mouth. It's all in the wrist; the way you move, sit, twist, and turn. You tell tales on yourself when you foot-jiggle, nibble on pencils, twist paper clips. Leaning into or away from people, sitting hunched up or relaxed are anatomical clues to your mind.

Silent language also gives you clues to other people's behavior. It is my firm belief that all behavior, conscious or unconscious, has a purpose. If you look for it, you can tell where a person's coming from. Everyone has infinite choices as to how he'll behave in a given situation. He chooses one. Why?

When you see somebody act in a way that doesn't seem quite right, before you react ask yourself, "What's the purpose?" A doctor friend of mine, Lucy, asked me that question about the chief of her surgical team. The hospital board had called in the team to justify its expenses. As Lucy was making her part of the presentation, she spotted the chief surgeon scowling and shaking his head. She was baffled. Why should he be against her? As I drew the story out of Lucy, his purpose became clear. The chief surgeon was on a spot. He'd had a history of run-ins with the board and needed to protect his position. He was trying to make himself look good by showing he was on their side; if anybody was remiss it had to be Lucy. I told her now that she understood what he wanted, she should have a talk with the chief and ask him not to make his brownie points at her expense.

Finding the purpose in somebody's behavior isn't always simple. When somebody sits there with a poker face you have to find out why. Maybe there's something he doesn't want to reveal. Maybe he wants to put you off base, or maybe he has a weak case. Maybe a poker face is all he has. Find out.

When somebody walks out on you in an unwarranted huff, look for the reason why. Is it to cause delay, create a crisis, shift the responsibility onto you? It could be something you said, or it could be a strategy. Find out. And deal with it.

You have to make a conscious effort to get at the real root of problems so you can use the right tactics to solve them.

Talking Back

An adversary screams in anger, raves like a madman. He or she is not angry or lunatic. It's just a person trying to tilt you off balance. Someone who has learned that people will often say or do anything just to snuff the flames of unsufferable frenzy. Don't play that game. Step back and assay the tumult objectively. Manufactured confusion is a technique to control you. Control back. Here are four techniques to detonate the screaming bombshell:

1. Outshout. If your opponent wants to get anywhere

with you, he or she will have to stop acting crazed long enough to hear what's on your mind.
2. Outtalk. Ignore the antics and keep talking in a conversational tone until he or she calms down or wears out. Then you can get on with a rational discussion.
3. Warn. Say if the tirade continues you'll walk out and there'll be nobody to agree or disagree with. Say if it keeps up you'll drive an extra-hard bargain.
4. Do the Drag-Walk. The dragged-out walk is an art. First you threaten to leave. Next, you collect your papers and paraphernalia. You get up. Then sit down and stand up again. If the harangue keeps on, you move toward the door and open it a crack. Still storming inside? Cross the threshold.. But don't race off into the night. Linger, in case you're called back. If you are not called back and you want the talk to go on, come back anyway. The dervish may have shot his or her load. A second swivet is not likely. Besides, you're apt to find him or her more cooperative after a walkout, relieved that you haven't abandoned ship.

Levin's Law: *All language is purposeful. To analyze and know the purpose of what people say gives you an added advantage.*

You have to learn to speak up on your own behalf and not let them outtalk you.

Four

Squaring Off: The Rites and Customs

TIGERS ARE EVERYWHERE. In the jungle they sniff and circle at the start of a fight—daring each other, testing, establishing who's who. People perform the same rituals. They strut, sashay, size each other up. They try to manipulate the conflict so it will end in their favor. Some are better at it than others.

It's a shame more people don't know how to start right. A lot rides on the opening gambits. How you position yourself early in the game establishes how you hold your ground once you're entangled. How you field curves can kill them before they kill you. If you maneuver right at the opening of a conflict, neither you nor the other guy will wind up with a torn throat.

Years of experience have taught me that certain patterns occur over and over again at the start of a disagreement. There is a system for handling them. The system works for other people and it will work for you. Once your understand the techniques, you will be in a better position to hold your own.

Steve, a friend of mine, is an account executive at an advertising agency. Everybody likes Steve. They see him as an agreeable, convivial, hard-working fellow who takes his job seriously and is fun to be with. Steve is also ambitious. He's in a competitive, high-pressure business, and knows that if he wants to be a star he has to be able to handle the people and situations he runs into better than anybody else. I tell him he'll succeed if he sees through the fast pace of advertising to the principles that underly any good business relationship.

I ran into Steve one afternoon on Madison Avenue. It was one of his nervous days: He was all jitters. Told me he'd just come from a new-business pitch the boss had assigned him to lead. He said he'd gone in armed to the teeth with thorough market research, a great dummy campaign, the whole dog-and-pony routine. What had him worried was he thought he'd come on too strong when he introduced the presentation. "I really gave it to them with both barrels and probably offended everybody in the room. I'm afraid I blew the account." I told Steve he'd done fine: Showing verbal muscle in opening speeches is a hallowed institution on the bargaining stage. Sometimes you have to play to the balcony. You let them know you intend to wage an epic campaign—it's going to be very tough, but you'll win it. In fact, you know that it won't be as tough as you say. Your ferocious stance is a dramatic device for the benefit of the agency people, or whomever you're representing. If you make what you're doing look extra-hard, they'll applaud when you succeed and forgive you for the points you lose. Your hype is an illusion that makes the people you're in conflict with feel good, too. You set yourself up as more formidable than you are. When you finally come to an agreement, they'll think they have been exceedingly clever to have performed well in the face of tremendous odds.

As I told Steve, opening theatrics are effective, but watch out for the built-in danger. You can start to believe your own lines and forget the realities when the argument goes into full swing. If you use histrionics, learn to keep them in their place. Know what's real and what isn't. Otherwise you'll be fighting with the wrong weapons.

Dressing for the Audience

Steve has a running battle with his clothes closet. He's never sure what to wear to the office or to a client meeting. He says his girl friend, Lisa, lectures that if he dresses too well he'll look pretentious, and if he dresses casually he'll look like a slob. He worries about making the right impression.

What I tell Steve is what I tell anybody who worries about how to dress: Appearances are messages. Know what you want to say.

You can show up in sweater and slacks at a meeting where everybody else is in a three-piece suit, and be packaged exactly right if your aim is to throw people off balance. Or you can wear jeans to play poor-boy. Your dress says, "I can't afford fancy four-hundred dollar suits. Obviously, I can't afford to play your high-priced game, either. It's plain that you're not going to be able to stick me for a lot of money in this deal." You have to be sure you know what you're doing. Odd-man-out packaging can also give the impression that you are arrogant, ignorant, independent, or overwhelmingly confident.

Most times, conventional clothing is best. You can always get down to being folksy if you decide that's what you want, and fling off the jacket or loosen your tie.

Most disagreements you get into are extemporaneous. They're touched off in an office, a cab, the dry cleaner's, at home. It's come as you are. In my business, I can always plan ahead for effect. Steve roared when I told him the dress trick I'm fond of using at late-night bargaining sessions. When I see that everyone is bedraggled and exhausted, I duck out, shower, change, and come back looking crisp and vinegary. It's a behavioral tactic. I come in refreshed and alert, and the opposition feels absolutely devastated by contrast.

How you dress can tell people where you stand. You need every possible advantage you can get.

Opening Statements Are Setups

One day Steve phoned to announce that he was a basket case. "I think I just walked into a propeller," he gasped. He told me he'd been called to a meeting with one of the agency's best clients, walked in with his usual cheerful grin, and got handed his head. For nothing, as far as he knew. Steve said, "The meeting started with the ad manager coming at me with unholy fire in his eye. He shrieked at me, 'You've been screwing us on this campaign and you're not going to get away with it anymore. If you think this meeting is going to go easily, you're crazy. Now let's get the show on the road in a hurry. I'm not going to waste any more of my time than I have to on this crummy campaign.' "

I told Steve he'd just had a lesson in firewater small talk, and not to take it personally. The ad manager was just letting off steam. He was also telegraphing that he was upset about something and taking it out on the first handy target. If Steve had a little more experience he wouldn't have taken the tirade at face value; he'd have heard it as a clue.

You have to go beyond the literal content of what you hear. Keep your antennae out for the real meaning of what it is people are broadcasting.

You can launch a disagreement in a friendly way,

be polite, equivocal, edgy, or out-and-out hostile. Take your pick. When you're on the receiving end, as Steve was, you have to understand what's really going on. Tough talk generally accomplishes one of four things:

1. *Catharsis.* Loud hisses to let off steam clear the air. Don't let them daunt you. People can build up a full head of anger and resentment just thinking about a fight. Let them get it off their chest. They'll be less vehement after their steam valves go off.

It doesn't hurt to let off steam yourself on occasion—as long as you don't overdo it or make it a habit.

You're apt to hear steam boil over during a disagreement, too. It builds up from the stress and frustrations of argument. Don't be alarmed. It's easy to cool the temperature down. Even a watery joke like "Don't confuse me with facts" can take the heat off.

2. *Flaunting Power.* Bragging, sanctimony, threatening to ruin you are more ways people let off steam. If it happens once or twice, let it pass; you can afford to. But stop anyone in his tracks who keeps on flogging you. The habit is as destructive as it is obnoxious.

Never tolerate abusiveness. Put the brakes on it fast. Hoodlums go in for calling names, hurling obscene insults, demanding you do menial chores for them. Stop. Pick yourself up and leave. If you want to come back and finish up the discussion later on, that's OK. Unless you're dealing with a psychotic, the abuse will probably be used up by then. It's hard for anyone to put on a wild-eyed act more than once.

3. *Warning.* Pay attention to red flags. They're to put you on guard that the disagreement you're in

is not going to go easily, and you'll need all your wits to get what you want. When you go in for a raise and the boss jumps your lines with, "There's going to be some belt-tightening around here. No more taxis, no more big-deal client lunches, no more padded expense accounts," he means, "I warn you, this is austerity time and it's going to be an uphill fight if you think you can get more money out of me."

4. *Emphasis.* Dramatics serve to underscore a message. You have to understand that they're just window dressing; fun, if you don't take them literally. Watch and learn. And brandish dramatics yourself when they emphasize your purpose. There's the old pound-on-the-table, shout-to-the-balcony routine. The terribly civilized, cool, level voice. Extravagance to make a point: "I've told you a hundred times I need a corner office." "You haven't taken me out to dinner in three years." "If you don't find me a hotel room I'll kill you."

Learn to read opening statements, not just hear them. They're hand-delivered messages that tell you what your opponents are up to. I assure you, they are trying to read your mind and maybe they can. You need all the information you can get to stay even.

You have to keep reminding yourself of Levin's Law of Language: It's a tool that can get you what you want—or kill you.

Be Sure You're Fighting with the Right Tiger

We were in a restaurant and Steve was fit to be tied. I said, "Stop trying to take it out on the steak, will you? Tell me what happened." He growled, "I am so frustrated I can't see straight. Today I spent two hours in a client's office discussing our advertising proposal with a guy, and I couldn't get him to make a single decision. He didn't OK it and he didn't say no. He wouldn't even suggest any changes he'd like us to make. I'm no better off than I was this morning, and the client has no campaign. What a waste of time!"

I said, "Steve, you got stuck with the wrong character. No wonder you couldn't win. If this guy has no new ideas, can't make changes, and can't make decisions, it's a safe bet he's just a puppet dancing to somebody else's rules. He has no authority. And he probably won't admit it."

There's no sense trying to wheel and deal with a vapor. You have to be sure you're talking with somebody who is able to make decisions and can back them up. Frilly titles don't mean a thing. The Executive Deputy to the President may be only a talking head, paralyzed when it comes to making a deal. You have to get to where the power is. Insist that you deal with people who can say yes or no. You wouldn't speak with an operator when you're hassling with the phone company over a bill; you'd go to the billing office, or higher. It's the same in any disagreement: If your puppet can't act, do an end run and get to somebody who can. Or else insist that whomever you're dealing with be vested with the authority to make and carry out decisions. At least, for as long as he's in a position to negotiate with you.

Levin's Law: *Never waste your time and energy in an argument with the wrong person. Nobody can win.*

At least when you talk to the right person you have a shot at getting what you want.

Sometimes you fight with the wrong tiger for a

different reason. Steve can't understand why sometimes an ad manager is belligerent and argues about
every ad he presents. He has to learn that the ad
manager has nothing to do with it. He's just following someone else's instructions. His boss has probably told him to come down hard on the agency so
the company will get it's money's worth. I tell Steve
to learn not to take the arguments personally, and
not to get roped into shouting back. It's better to
make friends with a puppet than to fight him. Get
him on your side and you can deal with the situation
as allies, not enemies. You add strength to your own
arguments when you include him in "Us against
them" instead of "Me versus you."

You may think you are fighting with your husband or wife, and it's really your mother-in-law
who's the cause of dissent. You may think you're
battling with your boss about a promotion, and not
be aware that the real problem is somebody else in
the office pressing him harder than you are. You
have to take the trouble to analyze who the real
enemy is. Recognize the difference between a puppet
and a tiger and at least you stand a chance to win
the scrap.

**Play with a Full Deck. And Deal Yourself the
Face Cards**

I get a kick out of Steve when he calls from the
office and says, "Let's meet for a drink after work."
I can tell he's having a terriffic day and wants to
share it. One evening we met for a drink and Steve
strode in licking cream off his whiskers. He was in
a rush to meet Lisa so he could show off a little, but
first he had to tell me. "There's a particularly hard-
nosed printer that the agency owes a lot of money

to. They'd be just right for a catalog I'm doing for a men's store, but I knew I'd have a hard time getting a good deal from them. The first thing I did, before the printer had a chance to hold me up, was call and say, 'I'd like to talk with you about doing a catalog for a men's store, but we can't do business unless you assure me there'll be no mention of our other billing with you.' It worked."

What Steve did was the same thing successful professional negotiators do. He seized the initiative and gave himself a prebargaining advantage by removing the printer's bargaining power before they began. He'd removed one pressure point by getting it out of the way beforehand. And he'd set himself up from the start as the one in charge of the situation.

Early birds get to pick the good worms. Stake your claim first and not many people will challenge you: It's easier for them to just go along. But use discretion. If you're overbearing or ask for too much, you'll only fan resistance and never get anywhere.

You can tell your boss you'll be glad to take on the the extra work he wants you to do, providing he gives you an open hand with the expenses that go with it. If he wants the work done, he'll agree to stay off your back. If he doesn't, you've tested and learned something else: Expenses are a problem your boss feels strongly about. Or maybe he doesn't think much of you. Or perhaps the job isn't very important.

You can tell the man who's repairing your hi-fi that you want to make it clear you won't pay his bill unless he delivers the set when he said he would. If he's late, getting paid is his problem, not yours. He'll probably deliver on time.

Levin's Law: *Take the initiative. It gives you a commanding position.*

Cosmetics to Make Things Look Good

Another way Steve could set up the printer so they would be affable about doing business with him is to ask them for little things, like memo pads at cost —extras that don't mean much to him or to them. I call these concessions "cosmetics." They make people think they look good. They've done you a favor, it doesn't cost them much, and they like you for accepting their help. Cosmetics make agreements look more like gifts in the end.

Don't be afraid to ask for trifles. If you don't get them, so what. They're unimportant and it's no skin off your nose. And be willing to make cosmetic concessions yourself. You're not giving up anything vital; you're making it easier to get what you want.

Thrusts and Parries, Promises and Threats

The threats you use at the start of a meeting are different from the bluffs you use in bargaining. They're a way to take people's temperature. When you're at the feeling-each-other-out stage, a little bullying can reveal the strengths and weaknesses you're facing.

You can show your own strength with a threat. Tell somebody you're about to dicker with, "Regardless of how this conversation comes out, whether we've settled on your fee or not, I'm leaving at five o'clock." You're letting him know your mind is made up: You don't intend to let him keep whacking away at your pocketbook. You are in charge. You don't really have to leave at 5:00 just because you said you would. Give yourself an out by adding, "If I see that we're making some headway, I'll stay a little longer."

This kind of talk takes the starch out of people. It shows you feel you are on solid ground and you're not going to take any nonsense. It gives you power. But think twice before you hurl threats:

1. Once you carry out a threat, you no longer have it. If the fee still isn't settled at 5:00 and you leave, then what? The other guy hasn't lost and you haven't won. Nothing's happened.
2. If you make threats and don't follow through, they won't take you seriously the next time. "Yeah," they'll say. "I've heard that one before." You'll be threatening into the wind.

Get the Talk Rolling: Big Issues Before Small

I've seen Steve in high gear, but this time took the cake. He'd heard a rumor that a big electronics account was up for grabs and he was in a lather, worrying about how he'd service an account that was ninety miles out of town. I put my hand on his shoulder. "Stop right there, Steve. First you have to make the pitch and get the account. Before that you have to cost it out at the agency. How do you know you can afford it even if you get it? And then, can you handle it? Who's going to write technical copy? Who's going to do the artwork?" I told Steve to think it through. "Tackle the big issues before you worry about small matters like transportation to the boondocks."

It's the same when you're in an argument. Start with the big issues and get them pounded out before you start hammering at the little ones. Once you've conquered the mountain, the hills will take care of themselves. And if you don't manage to plant your flag on the peak right away, you can always back down and start with the little pile, then swing back up to the top.

Some people feel if they get the little problems in a disagreement taken care of first, they can build on the momentum of having licked them, and crash to a grand finale. It is a preference, and whatever you are comfortable with is OK. The point is to recognize that you have the option of big things before small. Think it through and choose the strategy that works best at the moment.

How to Make a Habit of Getting OK's

I told Steve one way to win the account he's after is to toss out a string of sensible but innocuous marketing suggestions that are easy to say OK to. Sometimes you don't take risks right away; you get the ball rolling first. The idea is to get people into an agreeable frame of mind. Keep their heads bobbing up and down yes, and the habit may carry them right past a no. By the time you get to your big debatable question, it's easier for them to say OK than to start hassling with an agreeable person like you.

You've seen the theory at work a thousand times at home. The kids build you up with "Can I go play ball?"—OK. "Then can I watch television?"—OK. "And tonight, can we go out for dinner?"—Why not? People often use the technique to get extra work out of you: "Would you run off twenty-five copies of this report for me?"—OK. "While you're at it, will you type up an envelope for each one and get them into the mail tonight?"—OK. "And Ms. Patsy, on you way home will you drop this folder at the boss's house. It's not very far out of your way."

People may keep OKing you out of sheer relief that things are going more easily than they'd expected. I was visiting Steve's office one day and the receptionist, Sally, asked me what I thought she ought to do so she could get a day off for Christmas shopping. She explained that she wasn't on the best of terms with the office manager and was sure she'd get turned down if she asked straight out. I told Sally, "Make it easy for your office manager to give you the day off. The minute you say to her, 'I'd like to talk to you about something,' she's going to expect trouble. Surprise her. Ask for a string of little things that are easy for her to OK: 'Can we put some Christmas decorations in the reception room? Is it all right to have a small tree in the office? How about a little party Friday at the end of the day?' What you have asked was a cinch for your office manager to say OK to, and she will be feeling no pain. Ask for the Christmas shopping day next and I'll bet she OK's that, too. Why should she start a fight when everything's going so smoothly?"

Start by Asking for the Moon and Include the Stars

Part of the fun of being a professional bargainer is you know how to read between the lines. My civilian friends are always asking me what it really means when they read in the papers that a union is asking for ten or fifteen different things: wage increases, paid holidays, free health care, overtime, coffee breaks, more vacations—a galaxy of demands. "They're maniacs!" my friends exclaim. "They can't possibly expect to get all that. It's surreal. What do they think they're doing?"

I can tell you exactly what they are doing. They're performing the standard opening ritual of loading their case with extra demands they know they haven't a prayer of getting and don't really care about. You have to give yourself maneuvering space

when you bargain. The more you throw in—up to a
point—the more you have to give away. And the
more chance you have to have to get the things you
really want.

I was having lunch one day with Steve and Lisa.
She'd just found an apartment she wanted, but it was
in an old building and needed a good face-lift. Lisa
said the apartment absolutely had to have a complete
paint job, the cracks in the walls had to be fixed,
and the floors needed sanding. She was dejected.
She couldn't live in the apartment the way it was,
and she was pretty sure the landlord wouldn't take
care of the repairs. I turned over the lunch menu
and began to write:

> Paint entire apartment
> Repair cracks
> Install dishwasher
> Sand floors
> Smoke detectors
> New bathroom fixtures
> Build bookcases

I told Lisa to give the list to her landlord and
tell him these were the things she wanted before she
moved in. "Let him do some of the talking, Lisa, and
remember that there are just three things that are
essential and that he's likely to do."

Lisa phoned me a week later, bubbling. "The
apartment's a dream. I gave the landlord your list
and at first he yelped and crackled all over the place.
'What do you mean, build in bookcases? I never do
that for my tenants.' I said, 'All right, Mr. Green.
I'll forget about the bookcases if you'll take care of
the rest of the things on the list.' He roared, 'I'm not
going to remodel your bathroom! Do you know what
that would cost me? You'll just have to live with the

fixtures you've got.' I smiled my silkiest. 'Perhaps I can live with them. But only if you'll do the other things I've asked.' We went on like that and by the time we got through I had the paint, wall, and floor repairs guaranteed in writing. I'm so proud of myself. I feel like somebody who's driven a hard bargain, and it wasn't hard at all. But I'd never have gotten what I need without your list."

You have to learn to ask for more than you'll settle for if you want to get what you need. Not too much more, or none of your list will be believable. Enough to make them think they're getting away with something if they don't give it all to you. Start big and then come down to earth in bits and pieces, the way Lisa did, so you and they will inch closer and closer together and finally agree to what you need.

I think Lisa's experience taught her an important lesson in taking care of yourself:

Levin's Law: *To get what you want and deserve in life, you have to let people know that you expect to be treated well.*

You have to learn to stand up for your rights. And you have to do it so skillfully everyone wins.

What to Do with Excessive Demands
No amount of give-and-take will make people happy when your demands are excessive. To exaggerate so you'll have trade-offs is one thing. Being unreasonable out of greed or naïveté is another.

When you're the butt of bizarre demands, you can laugh them away or discredit them by pointing out the facts. Or do both at once. If Lisa had made the mistake of insisting that all seven improvements be made on the apartment or she wouldn't sign a lease, a smart landlord would have shot her down to size in a hurry. He'd have told her, "What you're asking for are things you should do yourself. Are you saying I should spend over three thousand dollars out of my own pocket? That's absurd. I'm in business to make money, not give it away."

Sometimes you can use ridicule and reality to get away with an oversize demand, as long as you're not wildly excessive. A free-lance copywriter friend of Steve's told a client that her price for writing a particular ad campaign would be $1,500. Her client said he was willing to pay $800. She answered, "At those rates I'd be working for a ridiculous hourly wage. You might get a hack for that kind of money, but not a good writer." Then she added, "I write fast and it'll probably only take me eight hours to do the ads. It would take anybody else four times that long, and the work wouldn't be as good. I'm a bargain, when you think about it." She exaggerated her estimate of working time in order to win her point, but stayed within the bounds of credibility. When the client challenged her, she could honestly say, "I may be off on my estimate of eight hours, but not by much."

Levin's Law: *Go into conflict with your eyes wide open and take advantage of every chance to gain the upper hand.*

If you recognize what opponents can do to you and are better and faster at it than they are, you can manage a disagreement so nobody gets hurt. You have to learn how to start right, so you don't lose before you have a chance to win.

Five

Preparation
for Battle

*T*HIS CHAPTER OUTLINES the checkpoints to cover before you plunge into a disagreement with your boss, your husband or wife, or whomever you are at odds with. Take the checkpoints seriously. They are the products of years of experience watching other people bang heads, and banging a few myself. Remember: Fools rush in—and stumble.

Understand the Principles of Problem Solving. They Will Never Fail You

Eighty percent of the people who call on me for advice could solve their own problems by using the formula I use at the bargaining table and in everyday life. I give it to you now in six clear steps.

1. Identify the problem.
2. List the relevant facts.
3. Restate the problem to include the relevant facts.
4. Freethink solutions.
5. Evaluate the conceivable solutions.
6. Select and implement the best solution(s).

Really carry out each step. Think hard and analyze the problem. Isolate and identify it in specific terms. Really make a list. Write it down. Be concrete. You can't solve a problem if you don't know what it's all about.

Remember my lawyer friend, Frank? He's been looking dejected lately. He told me he's unhappy in his work. Frank could reach a solution by using the six-step method.

1. *Identify the problem.* The problem is, should he change jobs?

2. *List the relevant facts.* There are too many bright young men on his level. Frank is not sure he can compete with all of them. He works at a large, prestigious firm. There are many advantages in terms of excellent resources, comfortable surroundings, security, valuable contacts, reputation-by-association. On the other hand, he may never be able to reach partner status there.

3. *Restate the problem to include the relevant facts.* Frank is not sure he can get ahead at the firm where he works. It's a large company that carries a lot of prestige. He may not be able to get another job with as prestigious a company, but he might get more money at another firm. He might get more interesting cases in a smaller firm, where he could practice in less specialized areas.

4. *Freethink solutions.* Frank could stay where he is and try to attract new business of his own, perhaps specializing in a field the firm does not now cover. He could talk to the head of the firm about his prospects there. He could look for a job elsewhere. Or he could start his own firm.

5. *Evaluate the conceivable solutions.* He could change jobs and earn a little more money, but in five years he might not be in as solid a position without a prestigious firm behind him. To start his own firm would take more time, money, and contacts than he could come up with. There is nothing to stop Frank

from going to the head of his firm and asking what his chances would be if he were to attract his own special clientele.

6. *Select and implement the best solution(s).* The best solution, obviously, is for Frank to forget his idea of changing jobs. He would be trading short-range financial benefits for the prestigious job he worked so hard to get. Perhaps by talking to the head of his firm and making it clear that he wants to get ahead—he'd be willing to work extra hours and entertain more—Frank could advance himself within the firm.

There is a risk attached to this solution. The risk is, the head of the firm can say, "Frank, you're really not as bright as all those other young men and perhaps the best thing is for you to start looking elsewhere." But even if this is the case, it would be a truth Frank would have to face sooner or later.

Levin's Law: *Success is understanding the system and using the tactics that give you a fighting chance.*

Check Your Early Warning System

With farsighted planning, you can abort a battle before it has a chance to begin. The minute you spot a crisis in the offing is the minute to go to work and eliminate it.

I'm sure you could cope with the problems of unemployment, an empty checkbook, divorce, if you had to. But why should you have to? Some problems need not happen at all. Look ahead. When your company installs a computer that will do away with your job, that's the time to get another job and avoid the problems of unemployment. If you see that everyone's overcharging you and you're not charging enough, change tactics before your bankroll hits the skids. You don't have to have one problem after another: Squelch them before they come up.

I have a friend, Greg, who is an architect. Greg is extremely talented, but not what you'd call a street fighter. His work is imaginative and distinctive, and he is building a fine reputation. He is proud of his work and feels he is in a very gratifying field. Except for one thing: getting paid. He can't understand why there is so much unpleasantness with clients over his bills. Most times he backs off from the arguments and settles for less than he should. Greg thinks it's not fair. He's right. Greg has to learn to anticipate that his bills are going to be questioned, and to do something about it so he won't keep having arguments about his fees. He has to understand that most people hate surprises, especially when money is involved. If Greg removed the surprise by giving his clients cost estimates in advance, they would have nothing to argue about when it came time to pay. You have to prepare people for what's coming, so any surprises will be pleasant ones. I've told Greg to get into the habit of submitting advance estimates and to make them higher than he thinks the final billing will be. Then when people get their actual bills, they'll think they are getting a bargain. Furthermore, if the actual bills happen to run as high as the puffed-up estimates, Greg's costs will be covered and he won't have to take a bath.

We are all tempted at times to bury our heads in the sand, hoping things will somehow work out so we won't have to face the music. The band always plays on.

Levin's Law: *Learn to look trouble in the eye early, before it gets out of hand.*

Realize Why People Miss Out: It's a State of Mind

I can understand why people think first of taking the direct and obvious route from A to Z when they negotiate, and neglect the fruitful bypaths. We are conditioned by ordinary everyday life to set win/ lose, yes or no goals. When you play golf, cards, baseball, any competitive game, the question never is, "What did the other person get out of it?" but "Did you win?" It's, "Did you get the job? Did you score on your date? Did you win the war?" And if you haven't gotten everything you went after, it's easier just to answer no than to come up with complicated explanations about what it was you did get. Explanations sound too much like excuses for not having won.

There are some people who can't bear anything less than an all-out victory when they are in conflict with us. They go the kamikaze route and push us to the wall until we collapse. They don't know enough to stop short of trouncing us. They don't realize that when they persist, they make us resist. Some way, some time, we'll look for a way to get even. They haven't won; they've bred trouble.

If somebody has been pushing you, you have to understand what is happening. You have to understand clearly that the process of productive bargaining is a two-way street. If you want to hold your own, you have to learn how to convey your messages firmly but in a way that does not put people down. If you call them names or punish them, they will do what all losers do: push back harder.

You have to learn to negotiate so that you make the other guy happy when you get what you want. The more clearly you understand how to maneuver people by thinking about what they need, the better off you will be.

Bring the Other Person into Your Head

When you have a problem that involves an adversary, the best process to use is to involve him in coming up with the solution.

The classic marital problem is when a husband and wife don't hear each other. "I've told you over and over, if you don't stop spending money I can't keep my head above water" is a standard. "You knew we had theater tickets for tonight, I said so at breakfast. Don't you ever listen to me?" The litany rolls on. You may be in the same situation yourself. Before you get complicated and start trying to work out the problem by devious techniques, I think it's important to know that you may not have a war on your hands—just a simple misunderstanding. People don't hear each other for a lot of reasons. They don't want to, they don't have to, they're concentrating on something else, your language conveys a different impression than what you'd intended. There are very simple rules to follow when you're trying to clarify a misunderstanding. They involve figuring it out together.

How to Solve a Simple Misunderstanding

1. State your position. Maybe the other person really doesn't know what it is, or didn't hear you right.

2. Ask him to play it back to you. That way you find out if he understood you. If not, you can clarify what he's misinterpreted.

3. Now state the other person's position, to be

sure you're clear about what he wants. Keep stating and clarifying until you're sure you're both in agreement.

4. With both positions clearly understood, you have a firm foundation for discussion and ideas. Now you can go on to construct a mutually agreeable solution. Or at least you can define the area where you are in serious disagreement.

Son of Bring-the-Other-Person-into-Your-Head

You can clear up a misunderstanding before an argument starts, but that doesn't mean it's forever. Misunderstandings often recur. People don't always listen attentively, or always say what they really mean. Whenever the idea "You don't hear a word I say" crops up, you're in trouble. Make it a rule, when that happens, to back up a paragraph before you foul yourself up any further. It's not a bad idea to do this periodically during an argument too, even when there is no sign of inattention. It's good insurance.

The rule is, follow rules 1 through 4 above: Before responding to a statement, each of you must summarize what he believes the other has just said. The speaker must agree that the summary is correct. Then you can proceed.

There's a side benefit to this rule that is one of the secrets of successful negotiating. Your summary becomes a reiteration of your position. The more often your position is stated, the more likely it is to be accepted.

And the more you show that you understand the other person's position, the more he will trust and cooperate with you.

The Power of Trust

You may think I'm being a Boy Scout, talking about the virtues when what you want to hear is bottom-line stuff. Hear me out. The virtue of trust is that it gets you to that bottom line.

Trust is what makes an opponent reveal things to you he'd otherwise conceal—inside information you can use to get what you want. Such as: A new contract will be in effect in thirty days, meaning staff changes are in the wind and you have a shot at a promotion. Or a big loan has just come through, meaning this is a good time to ask for a raise. Trust has its uses in practical ways.

I had a call not long ago from a woman I'd met in Chicago. She's the production director for a printer there. Very bright. Very good at her work. Very ambitious. She'd been offered a terrific job in production at a larger company in Southern California, and wanted to know what I thought about taking it. It would mean a big boost in salary, and she could swap Chicago's tough climate for days that were, as she said, "buttered with sunshine." The trouble is, she's heard a rumble that a conglomerate is getting ready to swallow the West Coast company. If that happens, her future in California may be less than sunny. Everybody knows there's a limited honeymoon for staff people when a new broom sweeps onto the scene. Nancy needs to get inside information so she can make a good decision.

I told Nancy to call her friend who is an executive officer on the Chicago Stock Exchange. He would let her in on the story. I reminded her that over the years they have exchanged confidential information many times. By now Nancy knows she can trust him to keep her question to himself. And he has learned that she has the judgment to protect him in the same way. He will respect her confidence and help solve her problem.

You need people with whom you have built mutual trust. The whole world is not out to get you. You can trust at least some of them to be on your side.

How to Build Trust

I probably don't have to tell you any of this. Or maybe I do, if it's something you haven't thought about. You build trust by showing that you'll come through in a jam. You keep your word. You follow through on promises. You don't take advantage of the other person's weak spots. You never blab confidences. In a business situation especially, you make sure you can back up any statement you make. You stay away from hyperbole. And whenever you can, you sneak in some useful and verifiable business news such as, "I hear Dave Diamond is going to open a jewelry store one block from yours." You show that you are knowledgeable, reliable, and ever helpful.

Levin's Law: *Work on building up trust. It is power when you need an ally.*

Know Thy Enemy

My architect friend, Greg, is always dealing with different kinds of clients. Some are reasonable, some are not. Sometimes he has to talk them into seeing things his way in order to get his work accepted. He says he always used to fly blind, hoping luck would be on his side. It rarely was. I'm teaching him that he has to do spadework beforehand, to be successful in selling his ideas.

One of the things you have to do before you get into any kind of fight is check out what kind of a fighter you're going to be facing. That way you can go in properly armed. Really size up the reason you're fighting with someone. Stop. Take time. Make a list of his characteristics. Where are the weak spots? Can he or she be flattered? Does he have to watch his step because of business or social connections? Who are his friends who could get to him for you? Could you get to him through public or political pressure? Maybe some deadline is swaying over his head and he can be pushed to a decision. His weaknesses can be your power.

Ask people he's done battle with before if he's a reasonable person or a nut. Does he play dirty? Find out if he's a drinker—and remember to order up a bucket of martinis for lunch. Or keep him away from the bar, if you want to do serious business.

Levin's Law: *You have to know who the enemy is before you can know the best strategy for holding your own against him.*

Check Your Backup Resources

As an architect, Greg often has to have backup for what he does. He needs proof that he knows what he's talking about. You may need it, too. Sometime during an argument you may have to pull evidence out of your sleeve to substantiate what you are saying. Think ahead, and have it with you. Dig up the documents that will help make your case: canceled checks, newspaper clips, government reports, industry statistics. Go to a library if you have to, or call on an expert for data. There are enough facts around to support any position you want to take. Nobody can argue with facts.

Checking on data can chew up your time. An option is to give the scut-work to somebody else. You can ask a friend or co-worker to dig into the files or make phone calls to get the information you need. Or invest a few dollars in a paid researcher. College library students like the experience as much as they welcome the cash.

One of the things you have to be prepared to do in a disagreement is be accurate. Otherwise you prove that you don't know what you are talking about, and your word means nothing. Take the trouble to be right.

Check Out the Bench Marks Beforehand

When an argument is going nowhere, you can get the stalled ball back into action by citing how others solved a similar problem. Your example adds another idea to work with. Furthermore, people are apt to go along with the precedent you bring up. "We could solve who we give tickets to on a first-come, first-served basis. That's what other clubs do and it works out fine."

Accountants practically live on precedents. I referred Florence, a hard-working insurance saleswoman, to an accountant when she got into a battle over travel-and-entertainment expenses. The accountant cited the allowances federal agencies give their employees, and gave Florence the added ammunition of T&E guidelines at comparable insurance companies. When she learned that average industry reimbursements were ten percent higher than she'd been getting—not the five percent she'd imagined—Florence waved the figures under her company's nose. She was ready to tell them, "Pay me what I ought to be getting or I'll go to another company that will." The argument never got that far. They brought her T&E into line when she showed the verified bench marks.

You have to make an effort if you want to get what is coming to you. Sometimes taking the trouble to find out what other people do is all the ammunition you need. You must take the trouble to dig for facts, analyze, and use them to your advantage.

Line Up Your Team

Some fights are plural. When you're in a group-on-group conflict, you need a strong team if you want to win the game. Give it forethought. You'll need a good balance of negotiating skills: some sweet mixed with the sour, and different points of view. People who all have the same attitude can all overlook the same dangers. Get both a hard-liner and a Mr. Nice Guy so that one can act tough when it's seat-belt time and the other can take the edge off the toughness. Have someone who sees the big picture and balance him with a good nit-picker. Have a historian to bolster your argument with facts and precedents. You don't need a huge chorus to have all the capabilities on tap. Most players can double or triple in brass.

You need an assortment of players in one-on-one arguments, too. When you're on your own, be your own team. Think of yourself as a one-person cast of characters: the nice guy, the hard-liner, the nit-picker, and so on. Perform mental acrobatics and switch roles whenever you need a particular expert. Being your own team is just another way of looking at yourself. It's a trick that makes you stronger when they come at you full force.

There's one more role you should know how to play: the character with no lines. Bring him on stage whenever you're tempted to babble more than you should. Anything you might sometime regret having said should never be said. Once you confide a secret, it's no longer your secret. It's everyone's information. They can use it to haunt you.

Intentional babbling is something else. Whispering your "secret" into a conduit's ear is a lovely way to plant an idea you want planted. It's also a good technique for convincing opponents of facts they wouldn't believe if they heard them from you.

My Turf or Yours

One of the critical, and controllable, elements of a fight is the battleground. Whose turf will we meet on, mine or yours? Which of us gets to choose the place? Why this room and not that? Very significant. A lot of strategic ice is cut over turf, especially when two sides are feeling each other out.

You can set yourself up as the person in control when you insist on "my turf."

You can give in and take their turf, then use the concession later as an IOU.

Or you can get into a tug-of-war over where to meet, and claw and scratch all the way to Armageddon.

The One-Upmanship of Turf

Why My Turf? My files are here. My reference books. My chair. My desk. I know where everything is and can use it without asking. My people are available if I need them. It's my command post.

Why Not My Turf? I don't want other people snooping around. My place is shabby. My facilities aren't the greatest. I can get up and leave whenever I want to.

Why Neutral Territory? Neutral ground is one way to cool a situation: It removes territorial advantage. If you meet in a club or hotel, you can keep phones, secretaries, and other distractions out of the scene.

Who Sits Where

Discussions take place at the bargaining table, in offices, living rooms, and in milady's chamber. The seating arrangements can be a serious matter.

In an office. The position of authority is behind the desk. I know I'm dealing with a smart person when I see him get up and walk around from time to time. He's making the others in the room think of him as a regular guy, not just self-appointed king of the hill.

In the living room. In a family quarrel, the seat of authority is usually the biggest chair in the room. Mamma and Pappa Bear can race to see who grabs it first, or contrive to leave it empty. One way is to preempt the chair with a pile of knitting needles, model airplane parts, or some other forbidding presence.

At the bargaining table. When you're dealing with groups, as I do, neither of the two leaders should ever be permitted to sit at the head of the table. That is automatically the position of control.

They must sit opposite one another, flanked by their lieutenants, rank opposite rank, on either side of the table.

Now you know why round tables were invented.

Take Advantage of Timing

There are morning people and there are night people. Some are bears until 11 A.M. Some start out frisky at dawn and fall apart by 4. Others feel either brisk or sluggish around the clock. It pays to know which type you're dealing with. Always remember: You must understand the nature of your opponent as well as the nature of the argument you're in, so you can be properly armed.

The first person to psyche is yourself. If you can set the time when you're going to thrash out the problem, make it for when you know you will be in peak form. The second person to psyche is your opponent. Take advantage of the other person's clockworks. You can get a remarkably fast decision out of people who want most in the world to go home and sleep. If they're smart, they won't let you pull that fast one. They'll say, "We'll talk again in the morning when my mind is fresh."

Use the pressure of time. Levin's Law: *Any discussion will completely fill the amount of time available.* Therefore, the shorter the time, the faster you'll wind up the argument. Don't let your meetings drag on; it's a waste. Limit sessions to one or two hours and you can wind up your talk in a hurry.

Turn time around. If people get the jump on you and set up a meeting time to their advantage, take over.

There are a number of ways to take charge. (1.) Refuse to meet at that hour. "Sorry. My therapy sessions are at eight." (2.) Invent a postponement. "It looks like I can't get there until after lunch. My car won't be fixed until one." (3.) Make your kind of time appealing. "Let's meet at my place Sunday at noon. We'll have coffee and cheesecake."

Never let yourself be boxed in. When you're told you must meet or make a decision in five minutes and you're not ready, don't do it. That five minutes could cost you more than making them wait five days while you regroup.

If you do get boxed in during an argument, don't let them push you. Give yourself thinking time. Nobody will kill you if you say you need a few minutes to think. The only trouble with that kind of time off is it makes you feel rushed. It's easier to stall by saying you have to make a phone call, use the bathroom, or skip out to a suddenly remembered appointment. Those are understandable delays. Everybody needs to use the phone or the john sometime, and nobody's going to hate you because you're due at the PTA. It's your business if you use the time to think things through.

Sometimes an argument starts to heat up just when you've said, "You'll have to excuse me. I have an appointment." You can always find a way to stay around and stick up for yourself. "The PTA can get along without me this once." "I can wait a while to make my call."

Levin's Law: *Use time and timing to your advantage. Never allow yourself to be stampeded into a decision.*

Prethink Your Objectives

Before you wade into battle, be very clear in your head what it is you want to end up with when it's

over. And be very clear about what you will settle
for if you don't get the sun and the moon.

If the fight is going to be about your salary,
know exactly how much you're after, and the least
that you will take. Do your homework. Guesstimates
can destroy you. You have to cost out all the specifics
ahead of time. What will you come out with after
taxes? What will you have to spend for transportation, phone calls, the galloping cost of living? Exactly what responsibilities are you taking on? What
salaries do other people get for your kind of work?
Can the boss afford to pay what you need to earn,
or are you being unrealistic?

Always remember the Levin Law that says: You
must go into situations with your eyes wide open,
so you can take the upper hand.

Frame Your Agenda

It is important to line up your argument before you
argue. For one thing, we all have slippery minds. It's
easy to forget something you'd meant to say when
you're caught in a rapid cross talk. Make yourself
prethink and write down the points you want to
cover. It will keep you from slipping out of gear.

Be strict with yourself. Otherwise you will drift
into digression after digression, and be caught in a
debate with no end. Focus on exactly what you want
to discuss, and don't let yourself be sidetracked from
your goal. You have to learn to stay on top of ycur-
self if you want to stay on top of everyone else.

Decide what you do not want to talk about, too.
You may have good reason to keep a point out of
contention. If so, make sure you keep it off the
agenda.

It is important to plan ahead so you know what you are doing. It is equally important not to be rigid. Leave your mind open, ready to latch onto any useful ideas that spring up during the conversation. And stay flexible enough to indulge in some purposeful sidetracking when you want to take your opponent's eye off the ball.

Remember this: A planned agenda is a framework for getting what you want. It is not a straitjacket.

Levin's Law: *Always keep your options open.*

Devise a Two-Sided Strategy

Take a hard look at the forces on both sides of your fight; the factors that will work for and against you. Obviously, you want to increase the forces that push things your way, and knock the stuffing out of whatever works against you.

It is axiomatic that if you push only for what you want, you will intensify your adversary's resistance. You have to think of the effect your demands will have on people. Go to the boss with, "I want a raise," and his immediate reaction will be to drum up every argument in the book against you.

The resistance syndrome is a universal reaction. To explain how it works, let's say that you go to your boss and ask for a raise. You can figure that your boss will immediately think of the money your raise will cost him. He will resist your request every way he can.

He may say that you are not worth more than you are getting.

He may say you are just using this job as a career stepping-stone.

What you should do is think through how he will resist before you go in and ask for more money. You have to anticipate opposition and create ways to counteract it.

You can show that you are worth more than you are getting. The dollars-and-cents evidence is, you brought in $12,000 worth of new business last year alone.

You can demonstrate your loyalty to the company by offering money-making ideas you would like to stay on and implement.

You have to take the steam out of resistance by working on other people's needs, not just your own. Make their needs work for, not against you.

When you think through your strategy beforehand, you predict how people will resist when you push. Then you can figure out how to counteract their resistance, so you get what you want.

Get into Foreplay. Seriously

The best of all ways to know what the real thing will be like is to try it out first. When you know an argument's coming, think it through in advance. Play out the dialogue. Act it out with a partner. Go through everything you are going to say, and rehearse how you will say it. Out loud. With a partner. When you have somebody to talk back to you, you have a way to get a foretaste of what your opponent will think and say. Then you can practice being fast on your mental feet.

You must keep in mind the Levin Law that you may not have a second chance. You have to be prepared to recognize opportunities immediately so you can leap on them and not lose out.

The Rules of Rehearsal

Act out every line with your partner playing the adversary. Go through the whole routine from start to finish. Take your foreplay seriously. No interrupting each other. No wisecracks. No horsing around. This argument means something to you, or you wouldn't be getting into it. Be ready for everything.

Make up several scenarios, and preview different ways the real battle could go. Swap roles with your partner, Let him be you and you be the person you'll fight with. You need to know what it is like to be in the enemy's shoes.

Critique each scene when it's over. Talk about what you did well and what needs tinkering up. Have a third person take notes, if you can. Were your facts flabby? Were you easily outwitted? Were your tactics so brilliant the other person was thrown for a loop?

It's at least as important to know where the enemy is coming from as it is to know where you're going. Full rehearsal will give you a leg up.

Put Yourself in the Other Person's Head

Before and during an argument, before and during any relationship that comes up, the art that can change your life is *the art of double-think.*

It's surprising to me how many people think in terms of their own message only. And wonder why they never get what they want. They are the simple-think people of the world.

A *simple-thinker* wants something, barges ahead and asks for it. He's baffled when he doesn't get it.

A *double-thinker* puts himself in other people's shoes. He uses empathy. He analyzes what's going on in people's minds. What is important to them? What are their needs? What pressures are on them? What makes them tick: their backgrounds, personalities, families.

A *triple-thinker* goes one further. He thinks, "What do people think when they put themselves in my shoes? What do they think that I think is important? How can I change their thinking, if it's not what I want them to think?"

I have a friend, Amy, who is a very successful authors' agent. She is a small, fragile woman with a stupendously intricate mind and the good sense to keep the intricacies hidden. Most people think she got to the top by being a nice person. Amy is successful because she is always one step ahead of everyone else.

One evening at dinner, Amy told me a double-think story I treasure. "One of my favorite clients recently completed a novel. The manuscript was rejected by three different publishing houses. Today I phoned the editor at a fourth house and asked if he wanted to see a brand-new novel by one of our leading literary figures." The dialogue went something like this:

EDITOR: No, Amy. I haven't got time to think about new material.

AMY: I know how rushed you are. I only called you because I know that Jack, the new head of your company, is interested in this author. I don't want Jack to feel he's being left out. Would you do this? Call Jack and let him know that we tried to bring the manuscript in to him.

EDITOR: Oh. Well, you know how much I respect your author. I'll try to make time to see the manuscript. When will you have it here?

AMY: I don't know when I can get it to you. Several other

editors have said they want to see it first, and one is reading it right now.

EDITOR: Amy, I really would like to give Jack a report as soon as possible. You said yourself . . .

AMY: Well, all right. Just promise me that you'll read the manuscript and get it back to me no later than Thursday.

Amy knew what was in the editor's mind. He knew it was important to maintain his standing with Jack. She knew the editor knew that Jack would think he was not doing his job if he missed out on this author. She used her ability to double-think to get what she wanted.

If the editor had been triple-thinking, he would have figured out Amy's ploy. But he still wouldn't have been able to do anything about it.

Amy says she always likes to be nice to people at their expense.

I promised you at the beginning of this book: *If you learn nothing else but to outthink your opponents, you will be far ahead of the game.*

The art of double-think can change your whole life.

Levin's Law: *Double-think makes a good bargainer. Triple-think makes a great one.*

Six

Tactics That Win

*T*HE BEST TACTICIANS are the people who grew up street-smart. They know how to defend themselves. They can outmaneuver anybody who tries to stab them in the back. They know all the tricks of making people who disagree with them come around to their way of thinking—and love it. They never let anyone box them into a corner. Watch their techniques. Add them to your repertoire.

The first rule is to remind yourself of Levin's Law and keep your options open. Be flexible. When one idea fails, search for other ways to get what you want. There is almost always at least one perfectly good alternative route. Often more.

Be open, but be smart. Never make the mistake of racing after every option that occurs to you. You could be racing to doomsday. Learn to use the six-step technique of problem solving. Weigh all of the alternatives before you plunge on. You have to look at the dangers as well as the benefits. Do the risks outweigh the advantages? Will you gain or lose more in the end? Can you find a way to combine alternative solutions, to get the best answer? Stop. Think it through.

The Yessable Proposition

> Levin's Law: *The more ways you give people to say yes to you, the more chances you have to get what you want.*

That law is the basis of successful bargaining. If you want to increase your chances to win, you have to know the system of Yessable Propositions. The system is this: Split up single issues into digestible portions. It's a matter of packaging. A Yessable Proposition gives people alternatives to simple yes-or-no answers. It gives them several ways to say yes.

Yessable Propositions open doors people gladly walk through.

Rigging a Yessable Proposition

To bring the enemy into your camp, you have to work on his needs as well as your own. One way to do this is to open up new bypaths with yessable alternatives.

My eighteen-year-old nephew Carl is a gangly, earnest type, inclined to be literal. Most of the time he has the look of a startled halibut. Carl is at the stage where he needs to be like the rest of the gang. He tries hard to do things he thinks people will like. He can't understand why they don't always see things his way.

Carl goes with a girl who is a born killjoy. He complains to me all the time. She doesn't want to go here, she doesn't want to do that. Whatever he suggests, she turns down. They were visiting me one night and Carl asked the Queen of the Vetoes if she'd like to go to a movie. She said no.

I couldn't let it pass. I inveigled Carl into the kitchen and gave him his first lesson in Yesmanship. I said, "Look, Carl. When you ask Susie if she'd like to go to a movie, there are two answers she can give you: yes or no. That gives you only a fifty-fifty chance of getting what you want. Why don't you weight the odds? If you say, 'Would you rather see the gangster film, the cowboy, or the comedy movie?' you give Susie three options to think about, besides turning you down. So you've got a seventy-five percent chance of her deciding on one of the movies, and only a twenty-five percent shot she'll say no."

Carl tried it out. Negative Sue said no to the cowboys, no to the gangsters, and OK to the comedy movie. They went and they had a good time. What's more important, Carl learned the trick of rigging a Yessable Proposition to get what he wants.

Yessable Propositions Are a Professional Tool

I got a letter a while ago from a former student of mine named Bernie. He's gone on to become a union representative and is still kind of green. He said he's been struggling with management, trying to get free dental care and prescriptions for his men. Management keeps turning him down. Bernie wanted to know what to do. I called him up and asked how he'd been presenting his request. He said, "First I asked them for a dental plan and they said, 'Out of the question.' I had to get some kind of benefit for my men, so I went back and asked them to provide free prescriptions. I couldn't believe it when they turned me down again."

"Bernie," I said, "remember all those class exercises when you learned to rig a proposition so it's multiple choice, to multiply your chances of getting an agreement? Now apply the principle outside the classroom. Here's what you do. Go back to management with a new, Yessable Proposition. Tell them your union wants either free dental care for themselves or free prescriptions for their families. And give them a third choice, to sweeten the pot. Tell them if they'll give you both the dental plan and the prescriptions, in exchange you will cut down on the number of personal days your men take off. Give them alternatives to consider, not just a yes or no. Make them think about which plan would be best —for them, not just for you. Let me know how it comes out."

Bernie's next letter was jubilant. He said he'd won both the dental plan and free prescriptions. And the company brass was actually happy about it. It wasn't hard to read between the lines. The third option Bernie came up with, exchanging days off for what his men wanted, meant the complete healthcare plan would almost pay for itself. The men were happy, management was happy, and Bernie was a hero.

You have to learn to think like a professional if you want to get professional results.

Playing on the Multiple-Choice Decision Process

The theory of decision making states that the process requires comparing alternatives. Think the theory through and you'll see that the *quality* of the alternatives you present counts as much as the *quantity*. Give people plenty of valuable alternatives and you'll get back plenty of answers you like. Here's how the game works:

A single proposition carries only one alternative: yes or no. A two-pronged proposition carries two alternatives to no: A or B. A three-pronged proposition carries three alternatives: A, B, or C. It gets even better when you look at the algebraic combinations: A and B; A, B, and C; and so on. Each progression increases the odds on the number of elements that will, by comparison with the others, be yessable.

The Yessable No

If you want to get really sophisticated with your yessables, try this. Add one absolute negative to your proposition—something they'll definitely say no to. By doing this, you add psychological power to the decision process and are even more likely to get a favorable answer. The negative item is a stalking horse. It draws attention to the three yessable alternatives by making a person have to consider which one of them is best. What happens to the negative is, it quietly fades away.

Try this one on for size. My friend Eleanor is an editor at a large publishing company. She was involved in putting together a book that she knew was bound to be a best seller. It was one of the pseudoserious self-help sex books. This was before sex was an acceptable literary subject: It was a daring publishing breakthrough. The book is still a runaway success.

The head of Eleanor's company is a woman who is an utter prude. Not only that, but she insists on having total approval of every book that goes out under her company imprint. Eleanor knew that when the woman took one look at the drawings in the sex book, she'd have a heart attack. There would be no way to get the book approved.

The book needed the illustrations, which were beautifully done. Eleanor called the author and asked if he could include thirty absolutely lewd photographs with his presentation. She assured him she had no intention of using them. She then submitted the entire package to the head of the company, along with a note saying how successful she thought the book would be, that she was sure the sales manager would handle it with great taste—and which illustrations do you want to use: the drawings or the photographs? It goes without saying . . .

I've seen plenty of bargainers, even professionals, who simply don't know how to go after a win. If they would use the basic yessable format, they could develop a yessable multi-issue proposition that takes the known no out of the picture completely.

Every time you go after something that you want, remind yourself of the basic bargaining law: The more ways you give people to say yes to you, the more chances you have to get what you want.

Stage Your Bouts in a Yessable Arena

It pays to mix business with pleasure. If this were Japan, I'd tell you to do as the Japanese do and make your deals in the baths. Here in the colonies, you can still manage to get your opponent comfortable and relaxed so he's feeling agreeable when you pop the proposition. Places like bars, restaurants, health clubs, and nineteenth holes are made-to-order settings. When was the last time you heard people shout and scream while savoring a sirloin, or when they relax after an exhausting game of squash?

Bill, a friend who's the president of a sneaker factory, asked me for help in settling a running battle he'd been having with one of his suppliers, a box manufacturer. This manufacturer was a pompous, irascible SOB and for months Bill had gotten nothing but grief from him. Meeting followed meeting and disagreement had followed disagreement. They needed each other but couldn't come to terms. I suggested to Bill that he take the steam out of the box maker by inviting him to sweat it out at the health club. Bill thought I was kidding, so I explained. In an office, the entire focus is on wheeling and dealing. But in the hedonistic atmosphere of a health club, business becomes incidental to working out and slumping in the sauna. The focus is softened and shoptalk becomes friendly chatter. It's a perfect place to clinch a deal.

There are other methods. I know salesmen who take their visiting regional managers on three-day sprees, and it works. They'll keep the manager drunk, bring in women, do whatever amounts to having whoopee. The manager thinks the salesman is a helluva fellow, and turns in a report designed to keep good-time Charlie very much with the company.

Mind you, I'm not recommending you bribe your way through business; I'm merely reporting what I've observed. There's more than meets the ear in "It's a pleasure to do business with you."

Small Things First

There's still the small-things-first school. This is not my game. But I'm not knocking it as a strategy. Those who play it swear by it, and it does have certain advantages. My Uncle Herb's friend Sarah plays it nearly every Saturday.

Sarah hasn't an evil bone in her body. She means well, keeps in touch with a covey of friends, and really dotes on my uncle. Incidentally, Sarah has plenty of money and has far more time and resources than Herb, who is an accountant with a wife, three children, and plenty of responsibilities. However, that does not stand in Sarah's way. Sarah's game is to call Herb up, very friendly, with a few things on her mind. How has he been, what's new in his life, she had a cold last week but she's fine now. By the way, she has a letter, a very short letter, that she has to get out. Could Herb's secretary type it for her?—Of course, Sarah. And would he mind picking up some stamps for her while he's out?—Certainly. I'm always glad to help out. Then comes the blockbuster, the thing Sarah really wants: Would Herb be a good fellow and drive her to see her friend in Brooklyn tomorrow?

What Sarah does is get Uncle Herb into the habit of agreeing to do a pile of inconsequential things, while she builds up to the crucial question. He never suspects a thing. Sarah is so nice and what she asks is so easy. She is setting Herb up so he feels good about being helpful. Then if he says no to the ride, he'll feel like a heel and blow his own image.

What Time Tomorrow Are You Coming to Move the Grand Piano?

Anyone who sets you up with a series of small demands leading to a larger one, or who makes trivia the issue rather than the big request, is making it very difficult for you. Here is what you do when you're in that spot. Use the technique used by professional bargainers: "Gee, I'd like to be able to help you but I can't do it tomorrow. My schedule is so busy right now I don't know when I'll be able to find the time." What professional bargainers say is, *Let's put it on the back burner.*

My Back Burner Runneth Over but It's All Right: There's Always the Shelf and the Table

I have put so many items on the back burner, shelved and tabled them in my time, it's a wonder people still go for the ploy. One reason they do is, it gives them a fabulous rush of relief. What it does for me is even better. It gives the other person time to think and realize that maybe he can't get what he wants and should try another tactic. And it keeps what could be a turndown off the official blotter.

This happens in business and bargaining every day. Of course, sometimes a rejection gets on the record before it can be headed off. When it does, I graciously decline acceptance. I say, "Let's put the whole subject on the back burner while you think about it. We can talk again in a day or two."

It's a stall technique that has various uses. Last summer one of my Long Island neighbors applied for a variance so he could build a swimming pool at his summer home. I got wind of the fact that the local zoning board was not going to grant the application and advised him to withdraw it instantly. That way, no rejection would be on his record. Meanwhile, we could ask around to find out the board's criteria and redesign his application to fit. He reapplied ninety days later, incorporating all the specs we'd unearthed, and got the variance without a hitch.

Drip Drip Drip: The Repetition Technique

People sometimes say no to a proposition just because you're feeding them a new idea. New ideas are hard to swallow. The way to make them go down is to soften the shock by repetition.

Once it was subversive to talk about U.S. trade with China. By now we've heard the idea so often we're used to it, and everybody's dying to get in on the act. The same thing happened with the social revolution of the sixties. I remember how appalled I was to learn that my niece was living with a young man. Out of wedlock, yet! By the time I'd heard the living-together story for the twentieth time and from a twentieth friend, the concept was perfectly acceptable to me. Look around. It's the same story everywhere. We wear jeans to restaurants, pay thirty-five cents for an apple, applaud nudity on Broadway. It all took getting used to.

Most people hate anything new. They'll fight it tooth and nail. You have to help them adjust to change, get them used to new ideas gradually. A friend of mine has a son, Brad, who used the drip tactic very successfully. He was planning to drive to California and explore life on the West Coast. As good a rapport as Brad had with his parents, he knew perfectly well that if he had just hit them with his plan, they would hit the ceiling. So he started to leave travel maps around the house. Mentioned that he was thinking of going to California. He was even smart enough to combine his dripping with a yessable tactic: "Gee, if I were out there, I'd like to go to school. I don't want to go to any eastern school, but I'd really like to study film making. All the best film schools are out there." And then later, "I think I'll drive by way of the southern route. Do you think I should take John or Mark with me?"

By the time Brad got through, the trip seemed a *fait accompli* to his parents and they were perfectly at ease with his plans. If he'd confronted them with

the idea out of nowhere, they might have said yes
—and probably no.

If you use the drip tactic, confine it to something you really want. When you belabor trivia,
you're just a pest. We all know people who keep
hammering away at petty stuff. They are a nuisance
and we wish they would go away.

Levin's Law: *The way to sell a new idea is to
remove the "new" by planting the idea again
and again until it roots.*

If somebody tries to drip drip drip on you, the
best defense is your trusty back burner. If you recognize the tactic fast enough, you may be able to shut
off the drip. Who wins this battle is largely a matter
of who has the greater will power.

Creative Vagueness

This is a tactic of making hazy statements that
sound inviting and are open to almost any interpreta-
tion. Masters of vagueness make their propositions
sound so attractive, whatever it is they've got you
want some too. They talk, they enthuse, they do
verbal arabesques. By the time they leave the room,
you have no idea what they've said.

Phil is a master. He is engaging to be with. A
great raconteur and an ace travel agent. He always
makes you feel good. Phil can spin a web of hazy
statements nobody can figure out or deny. Often he
uses vagueness to get people to do things his way.

Last summer Phil rented out his vacation home
and his sailboat along with it. Early in the season
he learned that his tenant had misused and damaged
the boat. Phil told him, "No more boat." The tenant

was up in arms. "You can't do that!" he screamed. "You leased the boat to me together with the house. We made a deal and you'll stick to it or I'm going to bring suit." Phil answered coolly and with not a seam showing, "You do what you have to do and I'll do what I have to do." Phil didn't say or threaten anything specific. He just left the tenant to worry it out for himself. Which he did. He had no idea what Phil meant, but it sounded ominous and his imagination made it worse. He gave up on the boat for the rest of the summer and never brought up the subject again.

Levin's Law: *Creative vagueness can be used to confuse the opposition while you create options for yourself.*

You can use creative vagueness for yourself in many situations. Phil uses it to mask flaws in vacation packages he sells: "You want a corner room, guaranteed? Don't worry about your room. I know this hotel and I have very good connections there. They'll treat you like royalty. Leave everything to me. You're going to have a fabulous trip. I'm starting you off with limousine service to the airport." They still don't know anything about their room, but it all sounds very good.

One way to defend yourself when you are the recipient of creative vagueness is to box the other person in. I overheard my nephew Carl, who is beginning to get the hang of dating, take care of himself in one of those exasperatingly vague situations.

CARL: Hi, Linda, would you like to go out for dinner with me Saturday night?

LINDA: Gee, I'd like to, Carl. But there are a few things hanging fire that I have to clear up before I can let you know.

CARL: When do you think you will know?

LINDA: Oh, maybe Friday night or Saturday morning.

Linda is being vague because an out-of-town boyfriend has said he's going to try to fly in and see her Saturday night.

Carl tries to pin Linda down.

The boyfriend said he'd call Friday morning, but Linda is taking no chances. She wants an out in case he's late calling.

CARL: I do have to make certain arrangements. Friday night or Saturday morning would be cutting it close. Could you let me know earlier? Thursday?

Carl isn't going to let himself be hung up till the last minute. If Linda can't make it, he wants time to ask somebody else for a date. He boxes Linda in with a deadline.

LINDA: I'll try, Carl, but it may not be possible. I'd really like to see you, but if I have to tell you on Thursday, I may have to say no just so I won't hold you up.

Linda tries buttering Carl up.

CARL: Linda, call me Thursday morning anyway and we'll take it from there.

Carl finishes boxing Linda in and opens up his options. If she's still giving him hazy answers on Thursday, he can either tell her he can't wait any longer and will see her another time, or give her another day to make up her mind.

Believable Threats

You use believable threats before you throw in the towel. When you think all has failed, stop. You have one more option, the threat. But you must use it with great care.

A friend of mine, Chris, manufactures small parts for airplanes. Right now he is a very worried man. He told me he has some large government contracts on the books, and he's desperate. He must get equipment capital so he can fill the orders and get paid. He says the bank that handles all of his accounts, which are considerable, turned him down on a loan. I told Chris to try pressuring the bank, but to be very cautious and make no commitments at first. "Start out vague, Chris. Don't give away your hand. Tell them if they can't come up with the money you need, you may have to start thinking about other banking alternatives. If they don't take the hint, then you can make your threat stronger. But be sure you can back it up." I told Chris to shop other banks in the area. If he gets any interest, he can honestly tell his own bank that he's talked to the XYZ National and they are working out the figures for him. He can tell them if they don't play ball, he'll take all of his accounts to XYZ. With several million dollars on the line, Chris's bank may be willing to talk business.

Be sure you remember the law about threats: the key is believability. If I were to threaten Muhammad Ali with a punch on the nose, it wouldn't move him at all. Let Sam Cunningham try it and the threat becomes real. If you want to be taken seriously, be sure you have muscle behind what you say.

And be sure that if you must follow through, your own neck won't be on the block. Ali wouldn't believe my threat. He'd know that the consequences to myself would be calamitous. If Chris threatens his bank, "Give me the loan or I'll close down my plant so you won't have my money to play with anymore," it wouldn't work. The bank knows Chris wants to fulfill those government contracts and see his business thrive.

In labor/management clashes, unions make their threats credible by setting up strike headquarters, by building strike funds, by printing picket signs. They show they mean business. A threatening nation bares its teeth by moving its troops to the border. On the home front, the husband or wife backs a threat to leave home by actually going out and leasing an apartment. A businessman who wants a loan from a supplier he owes money to, files bankruptcy papers to let it be known that he can't pay for supplies unless he gets the loan.

Use threats only when the issue is important, when you can't budge your opponent any other way, and when you are so far along in the conflict there is no other way.

Brinksmanship

This is a very high-level threat with long-lasting consequences. Brinksmanship is loaded with danger. It's like playing the game of Chicken: Unless you know that one car will steer away in time, it's all over. When you and someone you're fighting with are on a crash course—to divorce, the breakup of a partnership, a lawsuit, or some other terminal affair —resort to Brinksmanship only if you're sure one of you will pull away before the collision.

Brinksmanship is a threat that carries a heavy commitment. The Cuban missile tactic was serious Brinksmanship. President Kennedy committed our naval forces to intercept Russia's, as you recall. They were headed for Cuba and Kennedy had no time to sit around and strategize. He had to push the Russians to the brink fast. He warned them he was blockading Cuba and that the United States would turn back any ships that carried missiles to the island. For several days it was touch and go who would call whose hand first. Kennedy was determined not to back down, and he said so publicly. With the U.S. forces tensed on the brink, the Russians decided they had more to lose than to gain, and steered off course in time.

I suggested similar Brinksmanship a few years ago to the president of a construction company who was struggling to keep his business alive. This was during the last recession and things were very tight for Arthur. He needed $3 million to tide him over the coming four years. The bank that had been handling his accounts was pulling in its neck, and it being a recession, Arthur had nowhere else to go. I told him, "Before you do anything, you have to size up the situation. Is it possible for them to make you the loan? How strong are you? You have to really check it out. If you're on solid ground, you can push the bank to the brink and chances are you will get what you want. After all, they need your business for the long haul as much as you need them for immediate financing. It'll be hairy for a while, but I think it will work. At this point, you don't have much to lose."

I told Arthur to remind the bank president that if they didn't come through with the $3 million and he went under, they wouldn't get back their previous loans to him. It was him or them. Arthur told me later that the bank came up with enough to solve his most urgent problems.

Brinksmanship worked for Arthur. It is possible that it can work for you. But you must be very, very sure of what you are doing.

Levin's Law: *When you see that you have power, don't be afraid to use it.*

The Eisenhower Game

The Eisenhower Game is used to show that you are absolutely reasonable and will do anything you can. It disarms the other side.

General Eisenhower flashed this tactic in 1952 when he proclaimed, "I shall go to Korea to end the war." What he actually said was totally ambiguous and noncommittal, yet it changed the outcome of the Korean War and helped make Dwight David Eisenhower the thirty-fourth president of the United States.

To refresh your memory, Eisenhower ran for office in 1952, while the Korean War was dragging on. The incumbent president, Harry Truman, had decided not to run for reelection. His would-be Democratic successor was the eloquent Adlai Stevenson, who also had not come up with a way to stop the war. What Eisenhower's announcement did was underscore the Democrats' inactivity, and show America and the rest of the world that if elected *he* would be reasonable about talking peace.

The more you think about the Eisenhower Game the better it is. It has all the characteristics of creative vagueness. It gave Eisenhower time to maneuver while boxing the Democrats in: Their response must either be hawkish or me-too. It bought time with the Koreans, who had to decide whether the statement had muscle behind it or not. It put both the United States and the Republican party in a position of world leadership. It opened up the possibility of talks. And all the while, nobody had made any commitment whatsoever.

The Eisenhower Game is used in labor negotiations all the time. I recall that in one dispute a few years ago, a union had struck and the situation was deadlocked. Union funds were dwindling and the company, which up until that point held all the cards, refused to change its proposals. So the union issued a press release announcing that they were prepared to resume talks at any time with any appropriate company officials. Their game forced the company back to the table—they couldn't afford to look unreasonable—and opened the door to a settlement.

Making Power Out of Air

There are times when you are working in a vacuum. Nothing is happening, no one is reacting, you feel strongly about an issue and are powerless to move it along. A gem of a way to gain control is to create power out of thin air.

Walter, a friend of mine who is a professor at a small midwestern college, is the original Mr. Academia. He gets about as excited as the ivy on the college walls about world events. The truth is, he probably doesn't realize there *are* world events. His is a world of ancient Greek literature. When a new president came on campus last fall, Walter remained oblivious. Then he became conscious of loud rumblings. The new man on campus was hell-bent on revolutionizing the college. He was going to change the faculty's responsibilities, add to their teaching hours, remove their voting power. Walter was thoroughly alarmed. He called me to ask what I thought he should do. I reminded him of the law that you cannot do everything by yourself. I told him the only way he was going to stop the new president was to mobilize forces to support his position. I gave him a battle plan and he followed it to the letter.

Walter ran for office in the college senate, so he could have a voice. He wrote letters and made visits to professors at other colleges to find out what they had done in similar circumstances and to get their sympathy. He joined professional associations and got their backing along with their ideas. He called faculty meetings. He spoke out at assemblies. By the end of the winter term, Walter had rallied an enormous amount of support. In fact, he had become the leader. By May, he and his allies had enough power to stop the new president. There was no revolution.

Walter is currently on the receiving end of the power-out-of-thin-air tactic. His wife is obsessed with orchid-growing. Nothing will do until she gets a greenhouse built in their yard so she can indulge her passions properly. Walter told me that greenhouses cost a fortune and he can't see spending all that money on what he views as an indulgence. I happen to know that his wife has already begun to disarm him. She is working on her mother to talk to Walter about the joys of orchidology. She has enlisted Walter's sister to try to bring him around. She has their children enthused about the project: Most dinner-table conversations these days lean heavily toward Mother's hothouse. She even told

Walter she is talking to their bank about a home-improvement loan, just in case. With all those troops surrounding him—plus the threat of having to pay interest on a loan he really doesn't need—I believe Walter will give in.

Chipping Away

This is a process of sheer annoyance that, to my mind, degrades whoever does it. It works, though, and a good chipper can pile up a load of small items for himself just because the chippee wants to get rid of a nuisance.

You use chipping as a tactic when you don't have much bargaining power. Instead of lying down and getting nothing, you chip away at little things so that at least you can get a small share of what you want. You might not get the raise you're after, but if you keep pommeling away you could get a tiny boost in commissions—or Groundhog Day off with pay. Chip chip chip—until fatigue forces a small yes out of people, just to get rid of your infernal chipping. You take what you can get.

I am sure you have seen chipping in marital situations. It may even have happened to you. The classic is the wife who wants to have the whole house redecorated, and the husband who says "Nothing doing." She chips: "The living room lamps are a disgrace. Macy's has some pretty ones on sale this week. We'd better grab them while they're marked down." "Our dining room chairs are in shreds. I found this wonderful place where you can get slipcovers for a third of the price of reupholstering." By the time she's finished, the house looks half decent. It's better than no redecorating at all.

Don't Mention It and It Will Go Away

The other side of the chipper's repetitive pestering is *don't mention it.* Don't mention it and it will go away. Put an item on the back burner often enough and the steam will go out of the pot.

Chippers and Don't-Mention-Its are often wedded to each other, literally and figuratively. She keeps nagging and he keeps ignoring her. Often they are deadlocked forever.

The theory of Don't-Mention-It is that an issue becomes unimportant when it is not talked about.

Saying nothing has another advantage that makes it one of the most effective tactics you can use. Silence can make people chatter on and inadvertently support your position. People are always saying things that aren't good for them. Let them.

Does this scenario sound familiar? You tell your boss you need a raise because the cost of living is at Mach IV. He answers, "It's not anywhere near that bad. You don't need a raise." You let it pass, but you store what he said in your mental Rolodex. Sometime later when the boss says he can't afford this or that because "inflation's got me by the crotch," you snap smartly, "Ah ha! Just the other day you said inflation was no big deal. Now you say it is. You can't have it both ways."

Better Than Chipping

When you don't have much of a bargaining leg to stand on and you can't manage to get even small concessions by chipping away, roll over. Show your weakness. Deal from it. Appeal to your opponent's ethics. Who would pommel a sick, frail thing? Tell him you know he's a fair and honorable person; of course he'll be fair with you. Just be sure you're not rolling over for a killer.

People shove back to resist someone who is pushing at them. Conversely, they react mercifully to a confessed underdog. A subtly implied threat doesn't hurt, either. Underdeveloped nations use them all the time: "If you don't support us, the Communists will take over and then you'll be sorry." It works the same in business. In small companies anyway; big companies tend more to the shaft. The head of a firm that's in trouble will roll over and say to his staff, "I'm in a tight spot and I need your help. I have to ask you to take a cut in your commissions, or the company will go down the tube." If the staff likes the boss and he's been fair with them so far, they'll rally to keep the poor fellow from going under.

They may rally even if they hate him. They don't want to see their vested benefits, pension plans, and whatnot take a dive. The boss was counting on their self-interest when he rolled over.

Some people play underdog by dramatizing a limp, a cold, an operation, "nerves." They're looking for indulgence out of sympathy and they get it to a certain extent. Most of them overdo it.

Feigned Ire and Insanity

If there's one thing people will do almost anything to avert, it's blatant anger or craziness. Faced with rampant and frightening unpleasantness, they'll retreat, retrench, concede, do whatever will turn off the emotional spigots. Hitler ranted, the Germans kowtowed. Khrushchev pounded and the whole world heeded his shoe. A management representative I've watched for years trades on his penchant for getting down on all fours and beating the floor. Paul is about as crazy as a fox when he goes into his act: He knows perfectly well that people will do anything not to displease him further.

I'm a bit reluctant to tell you to use the technique of feigned madness. It must be expertly timed and controlled or you will simply break up your bargaining and make a fool of yourself besides. But if you know what you're doing—if you know your limits and can channel your strengths—go ahead.

Just remember that there is a difference between irrational behavior as a productive tactic and irrational behavior as a dirty trick. It's productive when people can come back with a useful, reasonable answer. It's a dirty trick when you act crazed on an irrelevant issue, and your purpose is only to stalemate the argument.

Deadline Devices

In bargaining, deadlines are not deadlines. They are tools for shaping an outcome. When your negotiation is flourishing, you don't break off the talk just because you've hit a deadline. You extend the time and keep on extending it until you've gotten what you want. "Let's talk one more time on Tuesday and get this thing ironed out. We're almost in agreement." Tuesday can roll into Thursday and Thursday into next week. But if you want a decision, you can't let time roll on forever. You have to tighten the noose; otherwise you will never bring home the bacon.

One of my neighbors, Charles, is a man who can belt out decisions the way a machine gun spits bullets. He is married to the most tentative person I know. Janet has trouble making up her mind about whether to get up in the morning. It drives Charles wild. He spoke to me about the problem recently. A long weekend was coming up and Charles wanted to get out of town. He said he didn't want to be cavalier about it; she complains enough that he runs her life. So he made Janet a Yessable Proposition. He asked whether she'd prefer a few days at East Hampton or a trip to Miami. Janet's answer was that both places sounded lovely to her; she couldn't make up her mind which she liked better. That's when Charles called me. He said, "I'm damned if I'll go through the week with everything up in the air. I love my wife but how do I get her to stop putzing around?" I told him to give Janet a deadline. "Tell her if she can't make up her mind by Tuesday, the trip is off and you'll stay home for the weekend."

Charles called me again Tuesday. "Would you believe it? Janet weaseled out of the deadline. She says Florida sounds wonderful to her, but she doesn't know yet if she can switch her Friday dentist appointment." I told Charles to pull in the reins. "Tell Janet she has until ten o'clock tomorrow morning and that's that." It worked. Janet stopped fooling around and they went to Florida. This shows the effectiveness of deadlines.

Another option, similiar to what legislators and football players do all the time, is to stop the clock. It is an option you can use in many situations. You can stop the clock for an indefinite period of time. If you see nothing is happening, you can threaten to start it ticking again toward the deadline. Then you can move people off the dime whenever you choose.

Sometimes short deadlines are essential, as in Brinksmanship and Believable Threats. A corollary to Levin's Law that any discussion will fill the time available is this: *The more time available, the more talk will take place. The more talk goes on, the less effective it becomes. Deadlines increase the momentum of any discussion.*

To be effective in any disagreement, you have to be as tactically smart as the next guy. If you have more tactics at your command than he, so much the better. You have the power to hold your own, and you will probably outmaneuver him besides.

Seven

The Split the Difference Proposition and Other Compromise Strategies

A DAY IS twenty-four hours and no longer. A yard is thirty-six inches, that's all. Some things you can't monkey around with: You have to divide what you've got. If you know what you're doing, you'll get your fair share.

Do not misread that word *compromise*. There is nothing wrong with it. Professional negotiators, international diplomats, and successful businessmen use it all the time. Look at it this way: If a share of the pie is all you can get, that's the best piece of pie in the world for you. It's when you wind up with less than your share that you have let yourself get kicked around.

I'll tell you something else about settling problems. Tactics and strategies that apply to one situation apply to another. The way you settle a gambling debt is the way you buy a house. The money you win in a horse race is the money you win in compromise.

The First Thing You Need Is a Manageable Conflict

As I've said before and emphasize now, the only way you'll ever arrive at a satisfying solution is if you're dealing with a manageable Type A conflict. Type B, with its veiled issues, will get you nowhere but into a tangle of troubles. If you think somebody's gripe is not what it appears, smoke out the real problem. If you think you have a problem and aren't getting the right answers, think it through. Maybe the trouble is you're asking the wrong questions. Face the realities. Be sure you are dealing with a genuine, manageable conflict. Then you can do something about it. There are dozens of ways to skin the cat.

You must constantly remind yourself of this Levin's Law: *You have to understand what your opponent wants and what you are willing to give. Otherwise you will just have a stalemate.*

Compromise Solutions: Six Propositions and What They Mean

A couple of years ago, my uncle by marriage, Ned, came to me with an engaging problem. He and his brother had been left acreage in Maine. The property had a couple of houses on it and two ponds. They both liked the place, but each had his own family. They were going to have to divide the land somehow. Ned wanted to make sure he didn't get the short end of the stick. He didn't want to start a feud with his brother, either. He asked me to help him figure out the best ways to get what was coming to him, and keep his brother happy too. The problem was so intriguing and had so many variations, I'm going to use it to illustrate the six most common compromises in settling disputes. They apply to almost any situation you will run into.

1. The Split the Difference Proposition
Let's say Ned and his brother Tom dickered over dividing the property and reached a stage where

each had a house and a pond. There was still wooded area left in the middle of the property. The woods could go with either lot. To reach a fair agreement, they could split the extra area and each would get half of the woods.

Splitting It Down the Middle. Splitting the difference is an extension of splitting it down the middle, a familiar compromise. It's what you do all the time with restaurant checks, chores, living quarters, time, and a million other everyday things. Ned and Tom could have halved all of the property in the first place and reached the same compromise they did by splitting the difference.

Like all of us, Ned has used the Split the Difference Proposition innumerable times to make a deal. I remember when he bought his house in New Jersey. The seller had started out sky-high, as most sellers do, and Ned started at rock bottom. They bargained each other up and down to where the numbers began to make sense. In the final round, the seller was stuck on $78,000 for the house and Ned's top offer was $76,000. They both wanted to wrap up the deal, so they agreed to split that last difference and settle on $77,000. It was an obvious, easy compromise that satisfied them both.

Splitting Intangibles. Ned and Tom could have compromised, without whacking up the property, by splitting its use. They and their families might have taken turns, one using the property in July and the other in August. They could have gone to Maine alternate summers. Or worked out some other fair division of time. They could have rented the property and shared the income.

Splitting intangibles isn't always that obvious.

One of my students stopped me one day after class. She looked wretched. She told me she was in a snarl that she couldn't unravel. Joanne and her sister owned a small ski house and were scrapping about who got to use it when. They each had the same brief winter vacations and each had her own set of friends. With one ski house between them, it just wasn't working out. They'd had another argument that morning. What could she do?

I pointed out to Joanne that there are certain things besides property that you can split: time, use, money, work loads. "Let's think about it for a minute, Joanne," I said. "If you and your sister sell the house furnished, you can split the profits. Then each of you can buy her own ski house and you'll have no more conflict. The way the real estate market is today, you'll probably both wind up with extra cash besides."

Levin's Law: *You can slice a compromise in many different ways.*

2. The Feels-Right Solution
Ned and Tom's property had an old path running north to south. It didn't exactly bisect the land, but it was close enough to the center so it formed a natural boundary. Dividing the property at the path would be acceptable to both brothers because it *felt* fair.

Paths, roads, rivers, mountains make good compromise divisions. They feel right. But you don't need nature to give you a boundary that's a natural. Look for other things that split.

Time. "Shall I come over at seven or eight? Oh, let's split the difference. I'll see you at seven-thirty."

Dates. "I'd like us to have a December wedding and you want it in June. Let's compromise and get married this March."

Locations. "If we build the new plant in Middleboro, the help from Boston and Cape Cod can both get there in reasonable traveling time."

Work Loads. "Sam, you take upstate New York, I'll cover Vermont and New Hampshire. It feels right in terms of travel and the number of accounts to cover."

Money. "Our joint tax refunds just came in. You take the federal refund, and I'll take the state and city refunds.

Rounding Off. "Let's round it off to an even number" is a compromise that gets the job done with no bones broken.

A research assistant used to keep sending me odd-numbered bills for his time and expenses: $176.18, $97.09. I was happy to give him a check for whatever he charged, but the figures were a nuisance to keep records of. I finally said, "Chet, wouldn't it be easier for you do what the government does on tax returns? Just round off your figures. You don't have to bill me for twenty-five minutes: Round it off to a half hour. I'm sure it would make your arithmetic simpler. And I'd much rather enter a check for ninety-eight dollars than ninety-seven dollars and nine cents."

3. Cut the Pie

I love this one because it involves double-think. One of the brothers, Ned or Tom, would divide the property. The other brother would take his choice of the two parcels. It's who cuts the pie that counts.

Always remember the law of double-think. It is

the difference between a good bargainer and a loser. If Ned cut the pie, he'd have to double-think. He'd have to put himself in Tom's mind and figure out what kind of parcels would appeal to Tom, so he'd be left with the lot he really wanted. It would work like this: Ned likes houses and he knows Tom is crazy about ponds. If Ned cuts the pie so one lot contains both ponds, he can bet Tom will pick that one and Ned will get the houses. But Ned will have to be very generous with the amount of land he assigns to the ponds. If Tom sees a stingy parcel, he'll figure he's being taken for a ride and will turn it down.

It takes a certain craftiness of mind and accuracy in double-think to cut the pie so you get the piece you want. Personally, I always want to be the one who does the cutting. It gives me control and options, especially when I'm sure of the other person's preference. I can decide what to include in each portion and rig the portions so I get the part I want.

When you double-think the other person and know how he will slice, or when you double-think and know that you both want the same thing, make sure he does the cutting. Then you'll get first pick and the best break.

You have to be very good at double-think to win at Cut-the-Pie. When you know for sure what's in people's minds, you can control who gets what.

The question of who cuts the pie came up at a postseminar bull session I attended last winter. The talk had roamed to personal chitchat and one of the other panelists was talking about his divorce. In addition to the usual horse-trading over alimony, house, car, and tax refunds, Larry and his wife were hassling over their art collection. He was very fond of most of the pieces and so was she. A few of the paintings that his wife raved about left Larry cold.

The question was, who was going to decide how to divide the paintings they both wanted. I told Larry to strategize: "You know that your wife is in a vacuum-cleaner mood over this divorce. She wants to walk off from the marriage with as much as she can, and clean you out if possible. Why not work on her mood, which amounts to greed, so you can at least get some of the paintings you want. Tell her you'll leave it up to her: She can divide the paintings into two separate collections and you'll pick the lot you want. She'll have to think hard. If she makes one lot meager and the other one fat, she can guess that you'll pick the fat one. So she probably won't do that. If she thinks harder, she might put the pictures that she thinks are wonderful, the ones you don't like, in a slightly smaller lot along with some of the paintings you both like. She'll count on you to be greedy enough to choose the larger lot and leave her favorites alone. I think you'll wind up getting what you want if you let her cut the pie. Even if it doesn't work, you can always trade certain paintings later. Never give up until you have exhausted every possibility."

4. Gambling
If Ned and Tom decided that one or the other should have all of the property and it didn't matter who got it, they could simply flip a coin. Or toss fingers. Or cut the cards. It would be a fair way to decide and it would be easy. It's the same way sandlot teams decide who's first up at bat. And the same way, I sometimes think, cops and headwaiters decide if they are going to be mean to you.

5. Use an Outsider
If it happened that Ned and Tom had very different ideas about dividing their property and they couldn't come to an agreement, their best bet would be to call in an outsider. It would have to be someone impartial and someone they both trusted. His job would be to decide which of their propositions was fairer. This technique in here-and-now problem solving has become the hottest thing in professional bargaining. It's called Last Offer Best Offer (LOBO). It works like this: Each of the dissenting parties writes up what he considers his last best offer and gives it in writing to the arbitrator/mediator. The arbitrator/mediator tries to help the two parties agree. If that doesn't work, he analyzes both proposals and decides which is the more reasonable.

In private life, you don't need a professional. Your mediator can be a lawyer, doctor, accountant, wise friend, or relative—anyone with no ax to grind and whom you and your opponent both trust.

The last-offer-best-offer technique is a beauty. It forces both sides to tailor their proposals so theirs will be the one the arbitrator/mediator picks. It also forces you to double-think. You have to figure out what the other person will put into *his* last best offer. You have to triple-think as well, to know what he expects you to put into yours. As a result of all this double- and triple-thinking, both LOBOs are very realistic. And because they are realistic, they are very close to each other. Because they are very close to each other, agreement comes readily.

6. Temporary Arrangements as Compromise
Like the common cold, many problems are self-limiting. It's a matter of time until they cure them-

selves. You don't need major surgery to take care of pain that will pass.

Sometimes a problem solves itself when a new product or service comes along. Calculators came along and solved the headache of forever being a penny off in your checkbook. Sometimes the passage of time brings new ideas to a situation. Or a larger, more pressing problem makes the first one fade away. You may be ready to bring suit against somebody who won't pay your $200 bill. Then your mother becomes ill and your mind is on more serious trouble than some small-time overdue account.

A temporary problem calls for a temporary solution. And that calls for an open mind and freewheeling imagination.

I have a friend, Sally, who used to work for a public relations firm in Dallas. She called one day to tell me that she had been offered a $22,000 job as public relations director of a hotel. She said she was dying to take the job, but she was on the horns of a dilemma. There was glamour and growing room in the hotel job, but she needed to earn $25,000. I told her, "You won't be stuck at twenty-two thousand for long if you do a good job. Why don't you think of that salary as temporary, and make it easy for the hotel people to take you on and give you a fast raise, too." I told Sally to make them a proposition. "Tell them you'll go to work at twenty-two thousand dollars, with the proviso that in six months you be raised to twenty-five thousand dollars if they're satisfied. If not, they can drop you from the payroll. Tell them you are willing to take the gamble out of hiring you."

It worked out perfectly. What Sally's proposal did was build a two-way incentive. She'd have to work her brains out to prove her $25,000 worth. And the hotel was motivated to take her on because they knew they could drop her with no hard feelings if she didn't pan out.

Temporary arrangements work well at the domestic level, too, as I'm sure you've observed. A live-in couple I know, Marge and Steve, told me one night that they'd locked horns over the cost of furnishing their four-room apartment. They couldn't agree on whether to buy what they could afford, which was the bare minimum, and live like monks or go into hock on their credit cards to furnish the place comfortably. "Hold it," I cautioned. "You're not married yet. You're living together to see how it works out. This situation is temporary and it calls for a temporary solution. Why don't you just rent furniture while you're living together. Then, if you decide to get married, you can go whole hog and buy for permanency. If you should split, you'll both come out clean. You'll have had the use of the furniture, your credit cards will be intact, and you won't get into a Lee Marvin courtroom scene over the sofa and chairs."

One of my frequent boat guests is the sales director of a large leasing company. When we first met last summer, Linda was still one of the sales staff. One afternoon, as we were sailing off Montauk, she told me she was being snowed by office politics. She was in line for promotion to sales director but the director of another division, a woman who hated Linda with a frenzy, was pulling every obscene trick in the book to destroy her. She'd launched a propaganda campaign to inflame the sales staff into telling management they didn't want Linda as their director. With that going on, even if Linda got the promotion, she'd be in a spot where her own staff would be against her. They'd make life miserable and see that she failed. Linda groaned, "I feel like that sail luffing. I can't move on. I might as well quit." I broke in: "Hold it, Linda. You haven't gotten where you are by being a quitter. You're going to get that promotion. You just have to outpolitic the Dragon Lady of Company Y. Here's what to do. Don't get yourself appointed sales director; get yourself named acting director. It's a temporary title that will do several things. It will end-run the woman who's trying to sink you. It will reduce opposition. It will put you in a position where you can prove your abilties. And it will give you a chance to establish a rapport with the sales staff. I'll bet you charm them over to your side within six months."

I knew I could bet on Linda. She's been sales director of the Y Leasing Company since February 1978.

Throwaways to Get What You Want

Bargaining is a seesaw game. It's a series of coming up and coming down in offers. You come up and I'll go down. You give me this and I'll give you that.

Some offers are built into a negotiation just for the sake of having something to give in on. They're expendables you can throw away when people accuse you of not playing ball. "Here," you can say. "Have one on me."

I went through a divorce by mail once with an old schoolmate, Tim. He and Margo were breaking up and it was no fun. They didn't want to become gladiators in a ring, so they were keeping the lawyers out of the act until they had decided how to split their belongings. Tim wrote me from Michigan that he'd like to bounce ideas off me, as a friend, so he wouldn't get taken over the coals.

"I don't want to hurt Margo," he wrote. "We both should get what's fair. But honestly, Ed, there's so much emotion attached to dividing property in a divorce, I'm not sure I know what's fair and what isn't. Or how to take care of myself if Margo should start listening to relatives and come on too strong. I'd appreciate your help."

Tim's letter went on to say that he'd told Margo he wanted to keep their car, boat, house, ski chalet, and have full-time custody of both children. "Of course, I can't handle all that," he wrote. "In fact, the reason I asked for the kids full time is so I'll have something to give in on later. Here's what Margo says she wants: Full custody of the children, the car, house, chalet, and one thousand dollars a week. She says I can have the boat. What do you think my next move should be?"

I wrote back to Tim that he'd done right to crank in things he knew he'd just as soon give up. I said, "You may have done this instinctively, Tim, but it was a twenty-four-carat professional strategem. Margo's already thrown in the towel on the boat. That means she can say, 'Look, I'm a reasonable woman. I already gave you the boat. You shouldn't deny me support.' The way I see it, your next step is to hold out for the house and give her half-time use of the chalet. Let her have the car, tell her you'll go to two hundred dollars a week support. And you still want full custody of the children."

Tim's second letter told me how that round went. Margo agreed to take half and give half of the chalet, but said she insisted on having the house and at least $750 a week support. She'd give in a little on the custody question by letting him have the children for two weeks of the year.

I could tell they were getting close to the wire and I wanted to make sure I was up to date on what was happening. And that Tim understood the game. I phoned him at his office right away and told him what I thought would work best. "Let's summarize, Tim. At this point Margo has the car, you have the boat, and each of you has half-use of the chalet. What's left to settle on is the house, financial support, and custody of the kids." Tim confirmed the score and I continued. "Tell Margo she can have the house until the kids are eighteen, then the ownership will revert to you. In return for your giving up the house for all those years, ask her to keep the support down to three hundred dollars a week and share the children fifty-fifty. Leave yourself open for more bargaining over your big throwaway, the children. I hate to call them throwaways, Tim, but that's why you're asking for more of them than you can handle, remember? So you'll have something to throw into the bargain."

It worked. Tim sent me a long and elated telegram outlining the final agreement.

MARGO HAS HOUSE TILL CHILDREN 18. THEN MINE AND PROBABLY WORTH MORE ON MARKET. CAN SWING $500 SUPPORT. KIDS MINE WEEKENDS AND SUMMERS. MARGO HAPPY. I'M HAPPY. GREAT COMPROMISE. PAINLESS DIVORCE.

Trade-Offs

A trade-off is a cousin to a throwaway. It's a tool for striking a compromise by swapping one thing for another. Tim and Margo traded off throwaways. Other people trade other things they consider to have equal value. It's common to trade off a raise for an expense account. One is taxable and the other isn't so an expense account can be worth as much or more in real dollars than a raise.

You have to keep an open mind when you make a deal, and figure out pluses for yourself that the other guy doesn't see.

Before you settle on a compromise, make sure you will get at least as much out of it as the other guy. You have to keep your options open about *how* you arrange your trade-offs, too. Sometimes you make out better by dealing in futures.

Stretched-Out Trade-Offs

I keep getting involved in my friends' divorces. Or at least, I keep being asked for advice. I often suggest a stretched-out trade-off as a creative way to reach a compromise divorce settlement. It's a way to leave both people satisfied, though I admit that word is either incongruent or redundant when used with "divorce."

Stretched-Out Alimony. For economic as well as social reasons, straight alimony is going out of style. With the ballooning cost of living, $800 a month can be worth a lot less than that a year from now, whether you're giving or getting it. One way to keep up with the dollar is to build in a cost-of-living escalator in trade for a low starting point. That gives the person who's paying a chance to regroup financially. And pray the payee will remarry before the escalator hits the ceiling.

Another version is to declare a two-year moratorium on alimony in trade for a healthy sum from then on.

Stretched-Out Property Settlement. My friend Jim phoned at eleven one night. He was frantic. He and Elsa were having an untidy divorce and she was trying to take him for everything. He yelled, "Dammit, she's not going to keep screwing me if I can help it. She's already got all the stocks, bonds, and bank accounts. Now she's going after the house. I won't let her get it. I bought it. I furnished it. It's mine and I'm going to keep it."

I said, "I sympathize with you, Jim. But Elsa's got you where she wants you. Now calm down. You can still come out of this healthy. Tell your lawyers to work out a deferred settlement on the house. Let Elsa have it, furnished, for as long as she remains single. The minute she remarries, the house will go back to you. You'll get her off your back and you'll still be building equity."

Jim was still anxious. "What if she doesn't remarry?"

"Fair question," I said. "I thought she had somebody in mind. Let's say that falls through. OK, let her have the house permanently . . ."

Jim went off the wall.

". . . providing she remarries within two years. Otherwise she loses the house. That will do two things for you. It'll get her to leave you alone for a couple of years. And it will push her into remarriage. You'll never have to pay alimony again. At least not to Elsa."

Sometimes the best way to get the best of a deal is to compromise. There are many different ways you can slice a pie. You have to learn to keep slicing until you get everything that is coming to you.

Levin's Law: *If you don't push as hard as you can, you'll never know how far you can go.*

Eight

Take It or Leave It and Other One-Sided Propositions

Dictators ride to and fro upon tigers which they dare not dismount. And the tigers are getting hungry.
—WINSTON CHURCHILL

THERE IS A certain type of person who gets his kicks out of being on top. This is the guy who needs a pigeon to prove he's the strongest kid on the block. He is a dictator: "You cannot do this. You may not have that. I will not give you what you want. Do what I tell you and don't argue." If you don't do everything his way, he won't play. With him, it's winner take all.

This business of the One-Sided Proposition is a bad bargain all around. It's no better for the person who tries to impose it than it is for the victim. When someone says, "Here's the deal—take it or leave it," he shuts off his own options. And he makes people resentful. You can be sure that somebody, somewhere, is trying to get even with him. A dictator is never beloved. In my book, the way he operates is no way to win a disagreement.

Just the same, I have seen too many people who let themselves get steamrollered by tyrants. It happens to them again and again. They think they have no choices. They are mistaken. You can make changes if you learn always to look for options.

Things *can* be different. You have to realize that it's OK to stand up and take care of yourself. Otherwise they will keep right on walking all over you.

What to Do When They're Bigger Than You Are

Some of the people who tell you "Take it or leave it" have the power to make their ultimatums stick. *Temporarily.* They are in charge of the company. There really is no money in the till for a raise. They will positively throw you out of the house if you don't buckle under.

You have to remember two things: There is always a next time, and nothing is forever. The pendulum always swings. The head of the company may be replaced. A budget can grow. They may find out that doing things their way isn't so great after all. You may think you have to take today's ultimatum, but tomorrow is apt to change everything. You are never stuck unless you allow yourself to be boxed in.

What you have to do is list every option you can think of, and weigh each one carefully. Think it through. Is it better for you to "take it," at least for a moment? Or would you be better off leaving. Which way would you gain more? Would taking cost more than it's worth? What will you lose if you drop the whole thing? What are your other options? How can you find a different way to handle the ultimatum so that you can get what you want—and leave the other guy smiling, too?

Just because somebody is bigger and has more power than you doesn't mean he's entitled to run your life. Your ideas may be better than his are.

Power Is a State of Mind

If you are one of those people who thinks you are always being walked all over, the reason may be that you don't realize how much power you have.

It may be that your own attitude is getting in your way. Do you cower reflexively whenever somebody barks at you? Keep reminding yourself not to take every shout personally. Often anger is the other person's problem. Do you habitually lie down and take the first thing people throw at you? What you have to do is remember to let them know that you intend to be treated well and will do everything possible to make sure that you are. Does the fact that there is a conflict scare you? Remind yourself every day of the law that conflict is opportunity. It is your chance to make the changes you want.

You have to stay on top of every situation. Take charge. Don't ever forget the law that says, It doesn't matter who you are or whom you are fighting with; once you know the tactics of successful bargaining, you can get the best of any deal.

When you find yourself in a take-it-or-leave-it situation, stop and analyze how you got there. You may have started in a conflict that could have gone to a 50-50 agreement, or a 60-40. Someplace along the line, did you let go of your power and let them take charge? Is that why you are losing out? Review the situation and figure it out, so next time you will be the one who stays in charge.

Some One-Sided Deals Aren't Worth Fighting About

I am not suggesting that you stand up and fight every order that comes down the line. General militancy gets you nowhere. You just wind up looking truculent and obnoxious. When you are dealing with trifles, let them go. Debates over nothing are a waste of time and emotion. If an edict comes down that you may not wear jeans at work, that's small change. Good sense says don't start an argument. You'd be smarter to say OK, and find another way to dress that will make both you and the boss comfortable.

I am a firm believer in my own motto, *Never back down.* But that doesn't mean you should start World War III over nothing. When a disagreement is unimportant, and they're not just trying to get the better of you, use good judgment. Let it pass.

Dictatorial Styles

Imperious, arbitrary types are certainly not hard to recognize. But it helps to know what makes them tick. Most people who need to dominate fall into one of the following categories:

The Executioner

This guy is a bruiser. He doesn't give a damn what you want. He's out for unconditional surrender. He will leave you with zero if he can. The executioner is a killer. His aim is raw power—damn the casualties and full steam ahead.

The Despot

The despot will leave you with something: whatever he is willing to give. He never thinks about your side of the deal. His line is, "I know you deserve a dollar but all I'm going to give you is fifty cents. Because I say so, that's why." Alternatives never occur to the despot.

The Autocrat

This is paternalism on the hoof, nineteenth-century style. The autocrat believes he is benevolent. He knows what is good for you. He will take care of you. But he will do it his way. The autocrat sermonizes, "I know you deserve a dollar. I could afford to give it to you. But that doesn't matter. What's right is for you to get fifty cents. Take it or leave it."

In professional bargaining, the autocratic style of domination is called Boulwarism, after the company labor negotiator who tried to make it stick. Back in the 1940s, Lemuel R. Boulware, a vice-president of the General Electric Company, got tired of the usual seesaw bargaining process. He figured he could short-circuit the whole business of negotiating if he did an intensive job of fact-finding and then decided what was fair for the unions to have. They would get what he knew was right. He was wrong.

Boulware gave Boulwarism a bad name because he ignored human nature. The union members figured if the company would give them what they wanted without haggling, what did they need a union for? The union leaders, enraged because they were being squeezed out, squeezed back. They screamed, "Unfair!" They brought lawsuits. They incited the workers. There were years of disruption over Boulwarism and the experiment proved a flop. That kind of paternalism has disappeared into labor's history books.

The Martyr, or Gandhi Effect

Martyrdom is a special order of usurpation by guilt. It is outrageous. It is beside the point. And it works. Look at Gandhi. He was the quintessential martyr. He set up Britain by threatening to starve himself to death unless they gave India its independence. And he put his threat where his mouth was, as it were. Gandhi fasted until he barely cast a shadow. If the British government hadn't caved in, his death would have been on their heads. Terminal guilt.

The martyr in everyday life one-ups you by always being in a worse position than you are. Whatever your problem is, he's undergoing something far worse. If you have pneumonia, he bleeds from the ulcer. If you have indigestion, he's off to the hospital with food poisoning. He will domineer you out of your mind if you let him. If you say you will leave him, he'll threaten to take an overdose and his death will be on your head. If you don't do what he says, his business will fail and it will be all your fault. His threats are so cosmic that you do what he says out of sheer scared-white guilt.

How They Get You

They say, "You'll be sorry"
People who are out to dominate try to scare you into submission. They threaten some horrendous consequences if you won't play the game their way. But sometimes they are just bluffing and can't back up their threats. They're like the wife who threatens to race home to mother, then invites dinner guests for the following day. Her bluff is as thin as glass. Next time she threatens to leave home, she'll be shooting with an empty gun.

The way to find out if a threat is just a bluff is to test it. Lift the veil and find out if there's anything real underneath. Try to offer other, yessable solutions. Use the what-if technique: "What if I help you pack and drive you to your mother's? Or would you rather talk out our differences?" If you make the right suggestions, you can open up doors for the other person as well as yourself. Keep reminding yourself that you have to confront real problems before you can get real answers.

They tell you, "What I say is final"
Dominating people are notorious for their wiles. A famous trick in bargaining is to say, "Here is my final offer, take it or leave it"—and then disappear. People who do this leave you with no one to argue with. And they run off with the advantage on their side. They say, "I'll give you two thousand dollars for your services. Let me know within forty-eight hours if you want to take it or not. We're not going to talk about it anymore because I'm on my way to catch a plane."

But that doesn't mean you are stuck. You can still make points for your side. Think of yourself as a winner, and create ways to get your message through. Chances are the guy who's gone off on a trip has told somebody where to reach him. Use that person to carry your message. If it's a secretary, tell him or her you have a terrific idea you're sure the boss will want to hear. Let the secretary relay your idea, along with word that the boss can reach you at home or in the office if he likes.

There's always a way out of what looks like an impasse. You just have to believe in yourself and make every effort to find it.

Let's continue the scenario about the disappearing customer. His response can tell you a lot. If he does telephone, you've opened up a way to talk. Follow through with everything you've got. If he doesn't call back, you've learned something else: He is determined to stick at $2,000. If he gets mad and backs off from you altogether, the gamble has cost you something. It means you didn't do your homework. You have to dig and find out the other person's problems so you handle them to your advantage. Learn to use your brain before you go barging into disaster.

It is true that you have to push for what you want, not lie down and take what they'll give you. If you never push, you'll never know how much you could gain. But you have to think through what you are doing carefully, beforehand. Stop before you push too hard: Figure out if you will risk more than you can gain. Never wade in unless your eyes are wide open.

Levin's Law: *In bargaining, everything is negotiable. It's the price you have to watch.*

How to Take Care of an Autocrat

People who try to dominate you have several large chinks in their armor. Those chinks can be your power. Look for the weak spots. Even if it seems small, it can be the edge you need. One frailty autocrats have is the need to be paternalistic. They have to be like Eisenhower and show that they are willing to sit down and talk. Their line is, "My door is always open. Come in and talk anytime." Play Eisenhower back to them. Go in and tell them, "You have such a fine reputation for being a reasonable human being. I am sure if we discuss this problem together, we can arrive at an intelligent solution."

You can appeal to their need to instruct. That need can be your opportunity. Pull them into an analysis of the facts. "Perhaps we should examine the background of this situation and see exactly what is at issue. Let's sort out the facts and see how they add up." They will be happy to play logician.

Trust their need to appear at least as decent as the next guy, and go with it. Autocrats are very civilized people. Use the technique back at them. Be extremely polite and calm. Point to standards of behavior. "I have heard there is a precedent for doing the sort of thing I suggest. Let me tell you about it and we can see if it fits our situation." Even when the autocrat is your husband or wife, you can say, "I have heard instances of how other couples work out problems like ours. There's one in particular I think we ought to consider."

An autocrat has to be parent, teacher, mentor, and gentleman. You can do him in on his own paternalistic turf. His weakness is your strength.

How to Take Care of Somebody Who Tells You, Take It or Leave It

A friend of mine named Andy is a road salesman for a toy manufacturer. He's been with the company for about three years and has outgrown his territory. Andy is bright, aggressive, and well-liked. He knows his business and I believe him when he tells me he could sell more toys if he had the big department stores to sell to. As it is, he's stuck with one small town after another and an account list of low-volume, mom-and-pop shops.

A little while ago, Andy went to his sales manager and asked for the Dallas-Houston area. He told me the sales manager turned him down flat and refused to give any reasons why. Andy can't understand what's going on. He says, "I want to improve myself. I know I can do better. How can I get the sales manager to listen to me?"

In this kind of situation the best ploy is probably the Eisenhower Game: "I will go anywhere and talk to anyone, anytime." You have to show that you will meet the other person more than halfway. That you will do everything you can to try to understand his point of view. That you are really interested in discussing his problems.

Once you have convinced him that you are sincere in your desire to cooperate, then you can make him a Yessable Proposition. Give him new ideas, choices to compare, alternatives to weigh. Increase the odds in your favor: Let him see that he can benefit by giving you what you want. Make him want to back off from his ultimatum.

If that doesn't work, use the power of time. Make it easy for him to try your idea. "Let's just experiment and do it this way for three months, and see how it works out." "Perhaps we can get someone else to cover the small accounts for the first year, while I'm cultivating the department stores. By that time, I may be able to handle both for you." Don't let him slam the door in your face. Put a wedge in, and keep the door open. "Let's talk again at the end of the season. You may have a reason to want to make changes then." That gives him an excuse to change his mind without losing face. And it gives you leverage to reopen the issue.

Anybody who won't tell you his reasons for giving you a take-it-or-leave-it answer is probably very unsure of himself. His insecurity is your power. Trust his frailty and go with it. He needs something to hold onto. All you have to do is make sure that "something" is you.

Fight Fire with Fire

Andy has another problem. He is in the market for a new car and has found the one he wants. Andy says, "There's one hitch. This car has all the options I'm looking for—tape deck, cushioned bucket seats—everything I need to be comfortable on my long trips. The basic price is five thousand dollars and the dealer wants an extra one thousand dollars on top of that. I know perfectly well he could throw in all the options for the five thousand dollars and still make a good profit. But I can't get him to budge. He knows he has the one car in town that I want. He has me where he wants me. He is one hard-nosed brute."

Andy's dealer is an executioner. He is out to get what he wants from the deal, period. He will try to shove it down Andy's throat and doesn't give a damn if Andy likes it or not.

Your best bet when you have to deal with an executioner is to ignore his tactics and do your own thing. First, do a stall. Say, "I'd like to go along with you and perhaps you are right. Give me a few days to think it over." Play the Eisenhower Game and be ever so agreeable about it—and ever so noncommittal.

While you are stalling, see if you can find out the cause of your problem. Maybe he is not serious. Maybe he isn't in the catbird seat after all. He may even change his mind. If he doesn't, you may have no choice but to go along with him.

The next step is to check out your options. There may be a different car that will satisfy you. You could find another dealer in another town who will play ball. Perhaps you can devise a counter offer that's too appealing to turn down. Check out all your options. Evaluate them. And do not give in until you have tried every way possible to get what you want.

If the executioner is your husband or wife, you may not have the time or desire to check out all your options. But you can still do a stall.

If none of this works, go to Brinksmanship. Drive the executioner right to the edge. Tell him if he wants to do business he'll have to see eye to eye with you or it's all over. Say you can do as well or better with somebody else, and give him backup proof that you can. Tell him he can take your proposition or leave it. Fight fire with fire.

Stall Them Off

I've heard a lot of take-it-or-leave-it propositions in my day, but the one my friend Karen just got has to be the most outrageous of them all. She called me one day to say that while she and her husband were having breakfast that morning, he'd suddenly put down the newspaper and announced that he was leaving her. Just like that. No argument. No discussion. He was fed up and he was leaving. He'd be back in the evening to pack. Poor Karen. I asked her if she'd had any idea this was coming. Did they have fights? Did he have a girl friend? Were they growing in different directions? There was nothing Karen could put her finger on and she was disconsolate. She loved the guy and he was about to walk out on her.

I told Karen she didn't have to take his announcement at face value. It wasn't necessarily a black-or-white proposition if she handled it right. "When he comes back tonight for his clothes, delay his move. Tell him you think he'll agree it's a good idea not to make a major decision without talking it through. Say, 'Let's give ourselves a week. That's not much, in a lifetime. During that week we can discuss our problem.' Be an Eisenhower: Tell him you will talk to him anytime, and you will do anything you can to save your marriage. Appeal to his reasonableness.

"Meantime, while you have that week's delay, collect your ideas and muster a Yessable Proposition.

You can suggest things you can do that will make life more pleasant. Offer to try a marriage counselor, to see if there's something about your relationship that you don't understand. You might propose a three-month trial separation, to get him out of feeling that he is trapped. He may find that living alone is not as much fun as he thought."

Even when you think it's all over because they've said it is, you still have the power to keep on negotiating. One way is to buy time. Make them realize they have nothing to lose if there's a delay. And make sure you use the delay for your own gain.

Drip Drip Drip. Get Them Used to Doing It Your Way

Another friend of mine, Ann, is one of those people who can't understand why they are always being taken. She has told me, "I guess I'm just a born loser. All my life I've done what I'm told. Even when I don't like it, I don't know how to stick up for myself. Anybody can steamroller me. Charles has me at the point where if he says, 'Jump,' I say 'How high?' He's in charge."

Ann was talking about her husband, whose latest tyranny was to put his foot down about where they would live. Charles is an anesthesiologist. At the time Ann called me, he was finishing his residency at a hospital in New York and had an offer to stay on. He'd also had offers from hospitals in other cities, which he refused to consider. Ann told me, "Charles was born and bred in New York. He thinks it's the only city in the world worth living in. But I'm a small-town girl. I've never been happy here and I can't see sacrificing the rest of my life to Charles's stubbornness. How can I get him to see things my way?"

I told Ann to use the old drip drip drip technique. "Get Charles used to the idea that there are other places to live. Get him to visit some smaller cities—Boston, Atlanta—so he can see what they look like. Introduce him to people you know there so he'll get a feeling of fitting in. Show him he won't die in the boondocks; call his attention to books and articles on the social and cultural life outside Manhattan. Turn yourself into a propaganda machine for the next several months. Get to him by sheer repetition. Talk about the good schools, the lower cost of living, the great golf courses in these other places. Charles may have told you he's put his foot down. Now get him used to moving it one step farther."

Use Guerrilla Tactics

I told Ann another way to tackle Charles's determination to stay in New York, with or without her: Wage counterwarfare. I said, "Defuse his tyranny. Show him he can't take you for granted. Cause a crisis so you'll have a chance to negotiate."

Ann was aghast. She said she couldn't believe I'd tell her to snipe away at her own husband. I pointed out that the purpose of sniping is to open Charles's eyes to something else he'd rather do. I said, "Pull your own power play. Stop taking his shirts to the laundry. Refuse to type his papers. Quit taking care of the family checking account. Show him what it will be like to get along on his own. When he sees what he'd be giving up, he may be more than willing to make a bargain with you. That's your chance to give him alternatives that will make you happy."

You have to accept the fact that power is there for the taking. It is yours once you have the attitude that nobody can domineer you unless you let them.

Pull Power Out of Thin Air

Ann has plenty of power at her command. She has to learn to reach out and use it. She can round up Charles's hospital colleagues and get them to bend his ear about the problems of living alone. She can get her friends and relations to pressure him about the advantages of smaller cities. She can ask Charles's mentor to give him the word about what will happen if he makes her miserable. The one thing Ann has to learn to *stop* doing is take Charles's decisions lying down.

You have to learn how to stand up for what you want. If you don't take care of yourself, who will?

Levin's Law: *Keep talking. You may find an opening.*

In any kind of bargaining situation, you have to make sure you keep on talking. Even if you think the other side will be furious at you for persisting, keep at it. The point is to keep the lines open so you can get them to negotiate with you. Otherwise you will spend the rest of your life letting them tell you what to do.

Fighting Back Against Domination

When people try to domineer you, they assume that they can. You have to assume they cannot. The great skill in fighting back starts with the attitude that you have more power than they have. You have to buy the fact that you are a winner and that you have power. Look for it. It is there to be had, even if you have to use your opponents' weak spots to get it.

Never be afraid to tell yourself that you hold all the cards. Once you learn to believe that, you will be in a position to act like a winner. You will be ready to pull out every winning defense in the book.

- Find out the reason behind their arbitrary statements.
- Work up a Yessable Proposition and give them a choice of benefits.
- Pull out the Eisenhower ploy and get them to talk reasonably.
- Do a stall. Keep the door open for further negotiations. Act as if they had not given an ultimatum.
- Drip drip drip. Get them used to doing it your way.
- Use Brinksmanship. Walk out if you must. Fight fire with fire.
- Take guerrilla action. Convince them it will be hard on them unless they make a good bargain with you.
- Call in outside help. Get other people to rally to your cause. Put on the counterpressure.

Levin's Law: *Always assume that you are just as smart and as strong as the people who try to steamroller you.*

Nine

Fighting
Dirty

... nothing is more fatal than a dodge. Wrongs may be forgiven, sufferings and losses will be forgiven or forgotten . . . but anything like chicanery, anything like a trick, will always rankle.

—WINSTON CHURCHILL

*W*E HAVE ALL* learned the hard way that there are rogues everywhere: artful dodgers who will pull any trick in the book to get what they want. They don't care who they pull their tricks on. You are as good a victim as anyone.

Yet we tend to forget there are people who are really out to get us. It's hard for us to believe that their intention actually is to do us dirt. We try to excuse them. We say, "It was an accident. He made a mistake. He was thoughtless. He didn't mean to hurt me, it just came out that way." You have to accept the fact that dirty tricks are not always accidental. There really are people whose prime goal and motivation is to get you. Make no mistake: They will ruin you if you let them.

I happen to be in a better spot than most to watch what goes on. If there's a way to throw a curve or work an angle, I assure you I've seen it. I can tell you this about dirty players: They may get the instant win, but what they win in the long run is usually distrust and scorn or revenge.

I am no moralist. In my line, I can't afford to be. I am simply pointing out that people who play dirty exist. You had better be able to spot them.

Games Tricksters Play

Lies, bribes, double deals, pimping—the tricks are a dime a dozen. So are their victims.

The Pedestal Setup

Flattery can be a poisonous flower. Nice to sniff; lethal if you swallow it. It can get a heel everywhere. He praises and fawns. Sets you up on a pedestal. Then with one swipe he knocks you down. Who can do it better? He built the monument. He put you up there. He is the one who can lay you low. The pedestal setup is a Judas kiss.

Louisa, a corporate attorney, told me this story. It happened when she was trying to negotiate a settlement for one of her clients.

I had to make the preliminary agreement with the opposing lawyer. He is a killer and very well known and highly respected in the field. I knew him by his reputation only. I was impressed and a bit intimidated by it.

I telephoned, and he got me in the first three sentences. "So this is Louisa. What a beautiful name. And I'll bet you're just as lovely as you sound." He had me. I was totally disarmed. Two sentences later he came back as a killer, but I was at a disadvantage. I was unable to reestablish myself as being just as tough and just as good a lawyer as he. He'd put me in a light that I either had to live up to or sound shoddy.

That man knew what he was doing. He set me up to be a nice person and I fell for it. Nobody will ever do that to me again. I'll know enough to tell anyone who tries setting me up that way to leave the baloney for social occasions and to get down to business. Or else I'll beat him at his own game. I'll put him up on such an absurdly tall pedestal that he'll understand I know what he's up to and that I don't intend to sit still for it.

Super-Civility
The terribly nice, monumentally civilized person belongs on murderer's row. He will kill you with politeness. He's a liar, a sneak, and a cheat. He will harass you from any angle, without regard for anything except what he's after. He behaves so beautifully that his victims wind up feeling guilty.

A liquor dealer I know, Jeff, told me how he was done in by a master of intricate civility.

I had a wine and liquor store that had been limping along for three or four years while I tried to build up a customer following and worked on getting deals from wholesalers. It was going too slowly. I had too little money and couldn't hold out a lot longer. What I needed was an injection of capital so I could beef up the business and make it pay.

About a year ago I met the person who could save me. It was a man who happened to come into the store one day. We fell into conversation and I found myself telling more than I'd meant to. Not that I blab to everybody off the street. But this person was obviously an extremely solid and sympathetic citizen. Saint Mark's, Grosse Point, and U.S. Steel rolled into one handsomely tailored, impeccably mannered gentleman. He was all kindness. We got as far as his learning that I was looking for a partner and he said, "My dear chap, there is nothing that would please me more than to see your business succeed. It happens to be an area I am very much interested in myself, and I will personally see to it that you are sufficiently financed. I would be grateful if you would permit me to become your partner."

This man was such a gentleman there was no way I could doubt his sincerity or turn away his proposal. It would have hurt his feelings. He even insisted on putting up not half but all of the thirty thousand dollars the business needed. When I demurred, he explained that it was all right. The thirty thousand dollars wasn't all his money, he had partners. He said he'd been looking for this very opportunity for years and please not to deny him his chance.

We signed a partnership agreement. His name would be on the company letterhead along with mine, and we would split the profits equally.

The man set it all up for me. He introduced me to his legal firm. Fine gentlemen. He personally took me around to meet the presidents of various wholesale companies and asked them to give me special consideration. He proposed me for membership in his country club so I would have the advantage of socializing with influential customers. I thought, "This man has class."

Then something strange began to happen. I had to go out of town for a couple of weeks and when I came back, I found that my office at the store had been preempted by one of my man's partners. He'd been told that I was no longer fully involved in the business and had made myself hard to get hold of lately. I also learned that my gentleman backer had gone to several of the wholesalers in my absence and advised them not to go all out on giving me breaks. He'd told them he was just trying to be kind to me.

When I asked what was going on, my "angel" said that everything was under control and not to worry. He suggested I take a long vacation or a leave of absence. Things were going so well I really wasn't needed in the business any longer.

You have to understand that all of this was done and said in such a way that it looked as if he were doing me favors. His conversations with our wholesalers and customers were the ultimate in decency, and he was courtesy incarnate to me. Nobody could fault the man or deny one thing he said. What he did was civilize me out of business.

The partnership agreement that seemed so well written doesn't mean a thing. My share of the profits is nowhere to be found. What is more, he has made it extremely hard for me to to do business with anyone in the liquor industry: They would think I was a raving lunatic if I told them why I can't go near the store or hinted that the man they know to be a gentleman is really a scoundrel.

What gripes me most is that it's my own damn fault. If I'd taken the trouble to check him out thoroughly and to scrutinize the agreement carefully, instead of being taken in by his superb manners, his air of decency, and his contacts, I wouldn't be in this mess.

Jeff is absolutely right about that. What he should have done was speak with a business adviser before he entered into any kind of a deal. He should have had his own lawyer check out the partnership agreement. He should have looked up people Mr. Civilized had done business with before. And if the good gentleman had objected or said, "That won't be necessary; you can trust me," Jeff should have seen that as a definite storm warning and turned his back on trouble before it began.

Harassment
Somehow the word sounds more innocent than it is. People who pull this dishonorable trick really hit below the belt. They work on you in such a way that you lead with your emotions instead of your brain. You can't fight back. They suck you into their webs and you're done for.

Don, a decorator friend of mine, fell prey to some hard-core harassment after he split up with his business partner.

I thought we'd made a clean break and would still be friends. We didn't dissolve the partnership over a quarrel. It was just a matter of convenience. I had my clientele, he had his, and we'd built up followings enough so we really didn't need the expense of retail space. We could each work out of our homes.

It was fine for about a year. My client list was growing and I thought his was, too. Whenever we'd meet for dinner he'd tell me he had a big job in Palm Beach or was going to do an installation in Mexico. Of course, he'd always been one for braggadocio, but I didn't take that into account at the time.

Then something weird started to happen. I'd go into the decorator's building and everybody would stop talking the minute I walked into the showroom. It was mortifying. I'd get phone calls at three in the morning and whoever it was would just breathe. I was beginning to be frightened and there was nothing I could do about it. I was depressed, too. My clients, the women who used to adore me, were giving me the cold shoulder. I didn't know why and they wouldn't tell me. Within six months my business shriveled like a caterpillar when somebody puts a match to it. Worst of all, I was hearing dreadful stories about my personal life, most of them untrue.

I couldn't figure out what I'd done to trigger this Machiavellian plot. Obviously, it was a plot. Or maybe I was getting paranoid as well as depressed.

I was having cocktails with a man who was my ex-partner's lover. He told me they were on the outs, about to break up. He also told me that my ex-partner had sworn to him six months ago that he was going to drive me out of the business in such a way that it would look as if I'd done it to myself. And then he was going to get every one of my clients for himself.

At this point it doesn't matter that what he's been telling people is wrong. The damage is done and it's going to take a long time to repair.

Don is right. The damage will be difficult to repair. What he can do is use counterharassment on his ex-partner. Now that he knows what is going on, he could keep his clients by fighting back on the same dirty turf. He could do the Mr. Civilized routine and say to his clients and resources, "You know, my former partner is going through a bad time. I hope you will understand and not think too badly of him. He seems to be losing his grip on reality. Maybe it's the medication he's on."

Terrorism

Some people have no superego. They don't care what people think of them. They are not afraid of scenes. They terrorize you because you know they will stop at nothing.

A surgeon friend of mine, Andy, went through a miserable marriage and a worse divorce. His ex-wife is a steel trap. Ice cold and merciless. Nothing fazes her. Andy says she'll never change. She is still after his blood. She is on a superharassment rampage in an effort to milk more money out of Andy.

When we went through the divorce I knew she'd carry on like a maniac if I showed up in the courtroom. I didn't dare contest a thing. Anything she wanted, she got. Now she wants more and she won't leave me alone, even though I've tried yessing her to death. She won't take yes for an answer. She wants cash and doesn't care what she does to make me give it to her. She has no compunction about barging into my office, no matter who's there, and harassing me. If I locked the door she'd just break it down. When she hears that I'm taking a woman to dinner, she invades the restaurant and attacks me in public. She's a Storm Trooper, a dreadnought. She'll stop at nothing until she gets me to cough up. Her latest trick left me bleeding. She marched into a patient's office and told stories about how I drank and beat her up when we were married. Needless to say, I lost a valuable patient. All I can do is get a court order that will put a legal restraint on her antics. And hope that she'll meet some guy who's fiercer than she is.

Out-and-Out Lies

Out-and-out lies are different from social lies, or distortions, or lies by omission. In professional bargaining, they're classed as a sin because they break down the negotiating process. You can't make a realistic settlement based on fiction. Out-and-out lies can be destructive in personal life, too. Unfortunately, they don't come with labels. It's very easy to be taken by a proficient liar.

It took Mary Lou eight years to find out she was married to a liar. They've since divorced and Mary Lou says she has learned not to be sucked in by anybody who is just trying to use her.

From the beginning, Matt was always cozy about everything he did. Who he saw for lunch, where he went after work, how much he earned. I never could get a clear answer. But I was in love with him and figured even though I was using up my trust fund in order to support us, it was worth it just to have him. It wasn't as if he were a gigolo, he said he just didn't have the money. He always swore that someday he'd be able to pay me back. And he'd buy me the clothes and vacations he wished he could give me now, too.

One day Matt's sister called me from Michigan, just to catch up on family news. She asked if I was enjoying our new island and what could she send me for a house gift. What island? What house? Maybe she'd gotten a story garbled. When Matt came home that night I asked him what she was talking about. He said he hadn't a clue.

About a month later, something came in the mail addressed to Matt. It was in a window envelope, so I knew it was a bill that I'd have to pay. I opened it, and it was a bill for property taxes—on Matt's house and island. Everything tumbled into place. The elusiveness about income and activities. The trips. The clothes and gadgets he said his brother sent him.

I gave Matt one more chance. I asked him again about the property. He denied it up and down and had the gall to demand proof.

I've quit being his patsy. I don't pay his bills any more. I know that his protestations about love have as much truth in them as his denials of income. I've thrown him out of the house and out of my life. Matt is the kind of guy who wants to grab everything and give nothing in return. I let him get away with it for a while, but now I'm standing up for my own rights. Next time I think I'm in love, I'll make sure it's not a one-sided deal.

The Awful Truth
Telling the truth can be as virulent as lying when the truth is meant to break bones. Remember Senator McCarthy's Senate-hearing assassinations? He killed people, based on what he claimed were "the facts." I've analyzed what McCarthy was up to. He fed his lust for power by coming on as the American public's best friend. Power, best friends, and the awful truth are often related. Remember ambitious Anne Baxter in *All About Eve*? You wanted to shake her teeth loose for telling Bette Davis those awful truths about how to take care of herself "for her own good." Only a best friend could have done it.

Cathy had a best friend. Or thought she did. She told me what happened.

Helen was my closest friend for years. She was my confidante. We talked at least twice a day. I told her everything. She knew the trouble Howard and I were having in our marriage, and was concerned about me. She sympathized, "Poor, Cathy. You've got to do something about it." She was wonderful. I was right there when she spoke to Howard and told him that the way he treated me wasn't right. He must go see a marriage counselor. She knew someone she was sure could help. When he wouldn't go and I was still having trouble with him, Helen urged me to get a lawyer. "You can't go on like this, Cathy. You'll ruin your health." She was so supportive, helping me get through a bad time.

I found out, after I saw a lawyer and went through with the divorce, that Helen and Howard had been having an affair for three years. They are now married. Helen got what she wanted: my husband. The experience taught me never to tell secrets that somebody can use as ammunition against me.

The Poor Innocent Me Ploy (PIMP)
Nixon put PIMP on the map, though he is certainly not the first or last to use this unsporting tactic. PIMPs victimize us every day. How many times have you heard the one about innocent me and the guilty computer? "Gee, I'd love to help you but our computer is on the fritz. My hands are tied." Go argue with a computer.

My attorney friend, Frank, says the partners in his law firm are working around the clock, trying to develop a case against an embezzler for one of their clients.

We can't find a way to make the charges stick, even though we're sure the defendant is guilty as sin. Every time we meet with him and his lawyers, or try to take a deposition, we can't get evidence we can use. We can't shake him from his story. He keeps repeating that he has no idea how ninety thousand dollars got put into the wrong account. It was other people's responsibility to keep track of the money. They did something wrong, not him. Then he weeps and says he's getting old and lame, only has a few years left. I tell you, if we do manage to get this case before a jury, we're going to have a hard time convincing them he's guilty. He'll have them sobbing into their handkerchiefs in the first hour of the trial.

You have to get a PIMP up against a wall before you can nail him. What Frank and his partners have to do is dig deep and marshal enough evidence so "poor innocent me" will have to pay back at least part of the money he lifted. They must be able to threaten him with jail, and be able to make the threat stick. They can get him into a position where they can say, "We'll drop the charges if you will restore the funds. Then you can save your precious reputation from being dragged in the dirt."

Intimidation by Insanity

Our old acquaintance, feigned anger or craziness, becomes a filthy trick when it's used to box people in. Its victims have no comeback. There's no way to reason directly with manufactured madness because its only purpose is to control you. What you have to do is work around it. My eighteen-year-old nephew's girl friend, Susie, is a victim of deliberate rage. It's the reason she always holds back from doing anything. Susie is afraid that anything she does will be wrong. She confided in me that her therapist says she's been set up by her father to mistrust her own judgment. He keeps her in tow by sheer fear.

Whatever I do, my father says I'm stupid. He flies into a rage if I do so much as ask to go to a movie. He goes absolutely purple and yells, "What's the matter with you! Don't you know any better? What do you think life is, fun?" Then, other times he acts sweet as pie. He'll take me to a movie himself. Or buy me a beautiful present. Just when I start to think I'm not so bad after all and maybe he likes me, he'll go berserk again. He swears and calls me names. Says all I ever do is cost him money and think about boys. You can hear the yelling halfway down the street. If I want to go to a movie when he's in that mood, I just don't ask. The trouble is, I never know what mood he's going to be in. I'm scared to do or say anything. It might start him up again.

Susie might be able to negotiate a peace treaty with her father so life would be more agreeable. She could create a crisis by going on strike. Next time he flies into an irrational rage she can refuse to go to school, take care of her room, or help with the dishes. The idea is to remove his ability to control her. Or she could line up the power she feels she lacks by getting her mother and anyone else who has influence to take her side. Susie has to learn to be resolute and hold her own in spite of her father's rages. If she keeps at it, eventually she can get him to sit down and talk rationally.

Double-Dealing Combined with Reneging
The expression *double-dealing* comes from the card-cheat's trick of dealing one card off the top and another off the bottom. He knows what he's doing but you don't. It's his invisible second game that gets you.

Jerry, the owner of a diner where I sometimes stop for coffee, told me he once took a shellacking from a double deal.

It was when we had our first child. My wife and I wanted to get out of our apartment into a house. We looked around and found the right house in the right neighborhood at the right price. Actually, the price stretched us to the limit. I hadn't been in business long enough to build up any reserves. But the broker assured us the property was in A-1 condition. It was brand new and I wouldn't have to sink money into a new furnace or roof repairs for a long time. We shook hands on the deal and we both signed a purchase and sale agreement. He gave me a few days to borrow the down payment from my brother and talk to my bank about mortgage terms. At the same time, I told my landlord we wouldn't be signing the lease that was coming up for renewal because we'd be moving within sixty days.

I had no problem borrowing money for the down payment or getting a mortgage from the bank. I was back at the real estate agent's office within forty-eight hours. The bum told me, "I tried to reach you by phone yesterday to head you off. Your phone must have been out of order." Like hell it was. He was just ducking a confrontation. What he'd done was sell the house for more money to somebody else he'd been dickering with all along. And left me out on a limb. When I pointed out that he'd signed a purchase-and-sale, he said, "So? It's only paper. Sue me if it makes you feel better. The lawyer will cost you more than it's worth." I wish I'd done my homework before I entered into any kind of an agreement. But I've learned my lesson. I'll never do business with anyone again until I've checked out his personal and professional references thoroughly.

There's another lesson in Jerry's shellacking. The real estate broker's fast shuffle is one of the oldest games in the book. It's sucker bait, designed to get you eager to make a buy and at the same time work you up to a higher price for the next thing that comes along.

Emotional Coercion
Coercion comes in many colors. Green when it's a payoff for keeping your mouth shut. Blush when sex is involved. Red when you are the angry victim.

Judy, a stockbroker I know, says she saw all three colors when it dawned on her that she'd been laid low, so to speak, by emotional coercion.

He was a client I was working very hard to get. He'd be worth an enormous amount to me in commissions. I did the usual, invited him as my guest to lunch and dinner. I knew he had the hots for me, but I've handled that trip before. It didn't bother me. Anyway, there was no temptation. He is definitely not my type.

I was this close to signing him on as my client. Then he put the pressure on. Romance was on his mind. He made it clear: no sex, no commissions. I think I panicked. I'd never had a client worth that much and I was scared to death the money would slip from my grasp if I didn't play ball. I suppose it's an old story, what I did, and I'm not terribly proud of it. But there you are. I was bludgeoned into bed, by a guy I don't even like. Yes, I still sleep with him. I still want those commissions.

Bribery and Payola

Bribery is the one dirty trick I have never actually witnessed taking place. It's the nature of bribery to be invisible. It's money passed under the table. Payola is more visible. It can look like mink, a Cadillac, a job, a kickback, or any one of the ways people buy favors.

Mac is a senior executive at an insurance agency, on his way to a vice-presidency. He says he'd expected the promotion a year and a half ago, and it's a miracle that he's getting it at all.

I was definitely in line for the vice-president slot. All of a sudden, the announcement came out: They'd given the promotion to Harry, another senior executive. I had no idea why but it wasn't fair. I'd worked hard and done all the right things. Then my own company betrayed me. I can tell you, I was depressed. My wife was none too happy, either.

The middle of last year, the SEC began an investigation of the company. And that's how I know why I didn't get the promotion when I should have. It all came out at the trial.

It seems that back in 1968 the president of the company had taken some personal interest-free loans from company funds, and Harry had helped him finagle it. They both knew this was shady—and heavy guns for the president if he was found out. So he told Harry that if he'd keep his mouth shut, he'd be raised to vice-president. Harry got the promotion as payola for covering up. And I got the shaft until the deal came to light. I suppose if I'd been more savvy I'd have realized that something fishy was going on when Harry got promoted for no good reason anybody could see.

Espionage

I know a lot of people who won't work in an office unless it has a file they can lock. Too many people would make hay out of their private notes and correspondence. They don't want their conversations stolen either. They talk on the phone as if there were Lilliputian spies inside the receiver. Why not; plenty of phones are bugged. They insist on soundproof walls, too. Much of the talk that goes on in an office has to be confidential.

Tight security means nothing when somebody's out to get you, as an acquaintance of mine was dismayed to learn. Bill is a television producer. He told me how he just missed out on hitting the big time because of foul play.

You have to visualize my office. It's upholstered, carpeted, and completely soundproof. And it's at the end of a corridor, well out of anyone's earshot.

I'd been holed up in there for two or three weeks, working on a sensational idea. A documentary series that, if I could sew up the details, would be a blockbuster. I was playing my cards very close to the chest. If any of the other producers knew what I was doing, they'd swipe the idea and I'd be out in the cold. I even had a hushing device put on my phone.

Somebody swiped the idea. I say "swiped." Every detail was identical, so coincidence is out of the question. It took me a while but I finally found out the insidious way they got hold of every word I said on the phone. A rival producer who works down the hall had hired a lip-reader as his secretary. I was a sitting duck.

Levin's Law: *You don't have to be paranoid to think somebody's out to get you. The truth is, plenty of people really mean to do you in.*

Don't be too quick to excuse someone who is doing rotten things to you. And don't be too quick to take it personally. What they're doing may have nothing to do with you. You may just happen to be the conduit for whatever it is they are after.

Learn to recognize a dirty trick for what it is.

And learn to fight back with every tactical weapon you can lay your hands on.

Ten

How to Wrap Up the Deal and Bring Home the Bacon

SOME PEOPLE DON'T know when they're ahead. They don't know when they should stop arguing and collect their win. When you have gotten what you want, you have to nail it down then and there. If you say, "I'll sleep on it and let you know tomorrow," you can bet your opponent will stay wide awake. When tomorrow comes he'll show up with sixteen bright ways to snatch the advantage out of your hands. You have to learn when to stop arguing and collect.

Some people lose out at the last minute because they get greedy. They have already pushed their opponent to the limit. Then they make the mistake of grabbing for more. They don't understand why they were within an ace of winning and wound up with zip.

You have to learn how to lock up an argument so it keeps going your way. Otherwise you will be back where you started. And somebody else will take home all the marbles.

Closing In on the Wrap-Up

When you see the light at the end of an argument, you don't rush up and slam the lid. You can get your fingers broken that way. Even at the very last minute, people will still try to take advantage of you. They will try to chisel you out of a little bit more. Do not let them. You have to learn to be as strategic when you wrap up a dispute as when you begin.

Keep Slush in Your Last Offer

A lot of people will turn down your final offer no matter how generous you make it sound. It's a familiar procedure. You may have gone through it yourself in buying a house. You go through the dickering routine and get the price down from $75,000. The seller holds out for $65,000 and you offer $60,000, knowing you could go another $10,000. He still holds out for $65,000 so you say, "Sixty thousand was my final offer, but you've talked me out of another five thousand dollars. All right, I'll give you sixty-five thousand dollars and that's it. If you want a deal, that's my absolutely final offer." You know you will go another $5,000 if you have to, but you hold it back. If the seller takes your $65,000, you're home. If he holds out for more, you still have some slush to play with.

I have often used the slush technique in professional negotiations. One of the times was when I was mediating a police department salary dispute. The committee members had agreed that a six percent increase was both fair and generous. They had also agreed that the police were in a mood to reject anything that was offered to them. If they'd been told two hours a week work and $1,000 a week for life, they'd have grumbled and turned it down. That six percent offer had to be made appealing, and the way to do it was to hold something back. I suggested to the negotiators that they offer a five percent increase. That way the police would have something to turn down and could get the orneriness out of their systems. That's exactly what happened. When we came back with the full six percent, they ratified it immediately and we locked up the agreement.

People will keep at you until they know there is no more in the cookie jar. You have to protect yourself and have two final offers to bargain with: your first one and your *final* final offer.

Final final offers give you an extra psychological advantage. They tell your opponents that you have really extended yourself to make them happy. It makes what you finally give more valuable.

You have to learn not to give away everything all at once. Even when you are down to the wire, you have to hold something back until the deal is sealed.

Levin's Law: *A good bargainer always keeps a little something extra to bargain with.*

Nothing Is Forever, Including Conclusions

People think they don't settle problems unless they have once-and-for-all guaranteed lifetime answers. They want permanent solutions for everything. To me that's like trying to cast clouds in concrete. Clouds change all the time and so do situations. Look around. They legislate permanent solutions to the energy problem and along comes solar energy to outdate the law. A couple carves out who gets which property, then changes its mind about divorce. A company fails, a friendship goes bust, new people come in and change the course of your life. Why lock yourself into a two-step? The orchestra may switch to a waltz. You must constantly bear in mind the law that teaches, Always keep your options open.

There is no such thing as insurance against uncertainty. You have to be flexible and ready to adjust to change. Look at it this way: An adjustable solution to a disagreement is like having pleats in your pants. It leaves room for change, space to adapt, and a way to avoid uncomfortable pressure.

Temporary Solutions
>"Let's try it for six months
>and see what happens."

The beauty of temporary solutions is they break down people's resistance to your proposals—they don't feel trapped by what you say. They think, "If this doesn't work out, in six months I'll be out of it with no hard feelings. It's not a life sentence."

Temporary solutions are an advantage on your side, too—you're not manacled to something forever. When something comes up that you hadn't foreseen, your escape hatch is ready and waiting.

Another advantage of temporary solutions is you can keep them around for as long as you want. How many "temporary" trial subscriptions to magazines have you renewed and kept on for a lifetime? How many times have you bought something "on appoval" and kept it permanently? Once people get used to a new idea, the idea becomes second skin—easy to keep right on wearing.

Delayed Action
>"Our agreement will go into effect
>five years from now."

Levin's Law: *The further away a starting point the less ominous it seems and the more readily it is accepted.*

If you don't have to start doing something you're not crazy about until the year 2000, you're not going to worry much about it now. Psychologists call this "approach avoidance." It's the reason most of us don't fret about 1985 emission standards; we figure something will happen by 1985 to change the rules. It's why we like credit cards and tax deferment plans; they won't cost us anything until later on. We are all Scarlett O'Hara under the skin.

When you delay the start of an agreement, you also remove a lot of the sting when the time comes to put it into effect. The arguing is over with; now it's an accepted fact of life. Remember the furor when they first started talking about a new traffic regulation? When the time came to put it into effect, you barely noticed the changeover.

Conditional Solutions
"If such and such happens, this
is what we will do."

There are two kinds of conditional solutions. In my business, we call them *reopener* and *formula* agreements. You use reopeners when you are not sure what will happen in the future to affect the agreement you make today. You say, "Let's talk again in six months about giving me a bigger raise. I expect to bring in some new accounts very soon." Reopener conditionals get people off the hook. The boss thinks he may never have to shell out the money for your raise. As for you, the reopener is an incentive. You'll break your neck to get those new accounts so you will be in a strong bargaining position six months from now.

Formula conditionals, or escalators, follow the "if" routine, too. But they are promises of sure things.

"If I bring in fifty thousand dollars in new businesss, I want a hundred dollars more a week. And another hundred dollars for every twenty-five thousand dollars' worth over that." "If the cost of living goes up, I want my salary to be increased proportionately."

Limited Solutions
"This agreement is limited to one year" (or to a certain amount of money, people, space, use, or other entity).

There are several advantages to clamping off an agreement at a certain point. One: Anything is easier to handle when there's an end in sight. When you know that a chore, a cost, an inconvenience will end at a definite and foreseeable time, you can put up with it while you have to. Two: A limitation keeps a once-bright idea from doddering into the sunset, useless and unloved. The whiz-bang solution for, say, controlling summer weekend traffic would be a drag if it was permitted to lap over into normal wintertime patterns. Three: Limiting something can keep costs from soaring out of hand. An experimental teaching method might be prohibitively expensive if it was used school-wide. By confining it to one department, you could prove or disprove the merits of the method economically. Four: Limiting an agreement limits people's ability to take advantage of you. Surely you would never loan your belongings to anybody on an ad-lib basis. You'd say, "You may take my car for the day." Or, "Use my apartment for the next ten days while I'm out of town." You have to be discriminating when you make a deal, even when it's with good friends.

Postponed Solutions
"Let's not do anything for now
and see what happens in six months."
Never underestimate the importance of doing
nothing. Action by inaction can be the smartest way
to sidestep complications. If every congressman re-
acted to every constituent who wants him to "do
something right away," we'd all drown in enact-
ments. Sometimes the strongest way to control a
situation is to make no agreement at all. You have
to know when to stay cool and not let them suck
you into hurting yourself. When you can see that
an agreement is no good for you, be firm. Make no
agreement. Let them wait until the situation eases
up or the problem takes care of itself. People will
nail you to the cross if you let them. You have to
learn to use your options.

Never let them paint you into a corner.

Making the Final Decision

There are as many ways to decide who gets what
as there are people to settle disputes with. Here is
a review of techniques you can use to get what is
coming to you.

Flip a Coin, Cut the Cards
When the earth won't move over who gets what or
who gets first choice, there's no sense arguing over
it. You might as well take the simple way out. The
odds on who wins the toss or the cut are fifty-fifty.
That's a fair and equal chance for both you and your
opponent.

Take a Vote
I don't know why people think a vote produces the right answer. Finding truth through democracy strikes me as a weird idea. However, you can use votes to settle a dispute. Even if the answer isn't the right one, it's a commonly accepted device for ending an argument.

Go for a Compromise
Cut the pie, split the difference, round off the numbers, settle on the natural feels-right solution. You can use any of the fair divisions we talked about in Chapter 7 as a good means to a compromise end.

The Let's-Get-It-Over-With Gambit
When you are in an argument that has dragged on and on and it's nothing but an endurance contest, get it over with. Settle for what you can get and get out.

You wouldn't be a Levin student if you didn't go one step farther. Before you settle and get out, make an effort to squeeze a little more out of the deal for yourself. Remember, your opponent wants to get it over with, too. He may give in just to put an end to the argument.

Always remember Levin's Law: Never quit trying until you are absolutely certain there is not one more thing you can do.

Lean on the Past
Precedent and past practice can be a pain when you're fighting with someone who relies on them as gospel. They can also be your tool for getting off dead center. "Everybody else gets fifty dollars an hour for this kind of work" can take care of a squab-

ble over your rates. "What Tim and Margo did smoothed out their problem nicely" can help settle your divorce difficulties. "You've always knocked ten percent off the price for me before. Let's just go along with the way you've been doing it."

When you lean on facts, you cut short a lot of needless haggling and argument.

Sweeten the Pot

Make it worthwhile for them to give you what you want: Promise them something aside from the main issue. A night on the town in return for signing your sales contract right away. An extra dozen of whatnots if they will wrap up the deal on the spot. Some extra something that is too sweet to resist can be the ingredient that settles the bargain.

Some call it seduction. I call it closing a deal.

When All Else Fails, Send for Help

When you have tried everything and still can't come to a decision, call in an outsider. Not just any outsider. Somebody you and your opponent respect, and a person you know is adept at solving your kind of problem. In professional bargaining, the third party is a mediator, fact finder, or arbitrator. In private life, your outsider can be a psychologist, clergyman, marriage counselor, pillar of the community, friend, relative, or an expert in your particular field. You can adapt the specifically defined roles professional outsiders play to get what you need from your own outside help.

Mediators. Mediators bring a fresh eye to stale problems and come up with solutions nobody else has thought of. I am often called into disputes where the answer is obvious the minute I step in; the people involved just haven't been able to see it.

In one dispute I mediated, one side was adamant about not giving information to the press and the other side insisted the public had a right to know what was going on. As the third neutral party, I was in a position to say I would be the one to inform the press whenever I judged there was information they should have.

In another dispute, my solution surprised both sides into agreeing with each other. Each had said they'd consider my recommendation, but neither wanted me to make any public announcement unless they were both in agreement. If the recommendation didn't go through, the side that rejected it would look like the bad guys. I said I would present my recommendation to each side, separately, before giving it to the press. Each side would have one hour to give me a note saying Accepted or Not Accepted. If I got two OK's, I would announce a settlement. If one or both sides said no go, I would make no announcement. One hour later, they handed me their notes. Both sides had accepted. They were finally in accord. What happened was, each party thought the other would say no. To be morally superior to the other, they each decided on acceptance.

Labor mediators do what outsiders do all the time. They take each party aside, clear away the frills, and get down to facts. They find out what each side really will settle for—just between themselves. And they are message bearers in the sense that old ideas sound fresh and respectable when they come from an outsider. They are good at holding up mirrors. They play back what the contestants have been doing and show them what the results can be. Often as not they just plain embarrass people into being reasonable. It's not easy to make outrageous statements in front of an outsider.

When more than two people are fighting, face-to-face negotiations are very tough. If two or three of the opponents agree, a fourth will dissent. A mediator can play shuttle diplomat and flit from party to party, getting facts here, making peace there, Kissingering them into harmony.

Fact Finders. Fact finders are just what they sound like: people who put the facts together and then recommend solutions.

In labor relations, a fact finder asks both sides to present all the facts they think are relevant. Then he sifts, weighs, and chooses those he thinks are the most important and works up a fair settlement. If a fact finder does his job right, both sides will complain about the solution. One thinks it's much too much, the other says it's not nearly enough.

Arbitrators. What an arbitrator does is listen to the facts and decide who's right and who's wrong. Then he makes a binding decision. It's as if the opponents hired a private judge to hand down a ruling they are pledged to abide by. In labor relations, arbitrators listen to the parties' testimony, examine their documents, take note of each side's arguments, and then write detailed reasoned opinions to support their decisions. Each side knows exactly why they won or lost, and the arbitrator's opinion can serve as the guideline in future disagreements.

This is probably more than you need in personal

conflict, but you can apply variations of the procedure. For instance, if you were fighting with somebody over what color to paint a room, you could
call in an arbitrator-decorator and go along with
whatever he or she says. Then if you don't like the
result, he or she gets the blame, not you.

A couple of new slants on professional arbitration
may interest you. There's the Last Offer Best Offer,
where both parties write up their LOBO's for the
arbitrator to read and choose between. And there
is Med-Arb. When somebody is called in to mediate
and mediation doesn't work, he switches over to
binding arbitration. Just the fact that he has the
power to make a binding decision gives the mediation more muscle.

Sewing It Up

You have to have a punctuation mark at the end of
an argument. Otherwise it just doesn't feel like the
end. How you write *finis* depends on the situation.
You can use a handshake, a kiss, or a signature
witnessed by notaries—anything that says The End,
peace at last.

Promises
You know what a promise is. It's a vow that you
will keep your agreement. Your word is as good
as you make it. You can't break a promise and expect
people to trust you the next time around. One broken
promise and you break down your relationship.

You have to remember when you sew up a deal
with a promise that you must keep your word.
Otherwise your word will be useless the next time.
There is always a next time.

Get It in Writing and Write It Yourself (IDIOT)
Details you think you will never forget can slip
from memory like snowflakes through a sieve. You
need a record of promises in a contract or letter of
agreement, so that people can't claim later, "That's
not what I meant." There is power in the written
word. There is more power when you write it yourself.

Levin's Law: *Once somebody offers you something, confirm it in writing.*

One of the best shows in labor relations comes
at the end of bargaining sessions. Both sides are exhausted. Their agreement still has to be put on
paper. The smart guy is the one who leaps into the
breach. He offers to write up the agreement, and
gives himself license to slide in subtle changes nobody has bargained for. I call this tactical "I'll do
it" offer the IDIOT, or I'll-Do-It-Ollie Technique.

Whoever does the writing can change details
in his favor: Switch a date, omit a comma, skip a
paragraph, slide in a phrase. It will slip by and the
other side will be stuck with the change.

I am by no means suggesting that you be
dishonest when you write up an agreement. I am
pointing out that (a) making the offer to write it up
can give you the upper hand, and (b) you have to
make sure the other guy doesn't do the writing and
switch meanings on you.

Always stay in charge. If you don't write the
agreement yourself, be sure you are in on the writing. The language of an agreement can make or
break you. Get it spelled out the way you want it.
If by chance somebody else does the writing, read it
through very carefully and tear it apart comma by
comma until you have what you want.

Side Letters
A side letter is just what it sounds like: a letter or memo of confirmation. "It is understood that you will bill me at three dollars and twenty-five cents each for orders of five thousand items or more. Should my order exceed twenty-five thousand, the price will be three dollars each." The side letter keeps your discount deal confidential, and gives you a written record if they try to renege.

You have to watch your step every inch of the way from start to finish when you are bargaining. You may be up against people who are shrewder than you are. Learn how to stay ahead of them. They will take advantage of you if you let them.

Eleven

The Power of
Levin's Laws

*L*IFE IS A conflict. It's a series of little wars that you have to identify, evaluate, and cope with. You have to establish yourself in life as a person who knows how to get what he or she wants. And you have to be skillful enough to make people like it. What you need is an iron fist in a velvet glove.

Learn the essentials. Use them every day of your life. The more you use them, the more skilled you will become. It is the only way you will ever be able to take care of yourself successfully.

It's time you took charge of your life. The secrets are these:

- Use conflict as your opportunity to make changes.
- Analyze what it is possible for you to get.
- Know whom you are dealing with.
- Know what you are fighting about.
- Really do your homework.
- Learn to take the initiative.
- Learn to double- and triple-think your opponents.
- Once you see that you have power, bear down and use it.
- Invent new ways to get what you want.
- Give people choices they will want to agree to.
- Leap into every opportunity. You may not get a second chance.

- Learn how to leave everyone happy.
- Never take a loss personally.
- Always keep your options open.
- Never stop trying to win.

The system works. It works for others and it will work for you. Use it, and make the changes you want in your life.

You *can* have the last laugh.